THE
GILBERT
and
SULLIVAN
OPERAS

THE GILBERT and SULLIVAN OPERAS

DARLENE GEIS

HARRY N. ABRAMS, INC., PUBLISHERS, NEW YORK

Frontispiece: *Major-General Stanley and his daughters on the rocky coast of Penzance.*

Copy Editor: *Donn Teal*
Designer: *Betty Binns Graphics*

Library of Congress Cataloging in Publication Data

Geis, Darlene.
   The Gilbert and Sullivan operas.

   1. Gilbert, William Schwenck, Sir, 1836–1911.
2. Sullivan, Arthur Seymour, Sir, 1842–1900. Operas.
I. Title.
ML410.S95G44   1983   782.81′092′4   83–2582
ISBN 0-8109-0984-7

Illustrations ©*1983 Harry N. Abrams, Inc.*

Published in 1983 by Harry N. Abrams, Incorporated, New York

Printed and bound in Japan

CONTENTS

PERFORMED AT THE PROMENADE CONCERTS,
COVENT GARDEN THEATRE.
BY
CHARLES COOTE JUN.ᴿ

OVERTURE

In 1869 the curtain rose on the prologue to the greatest partnership in the English musical theater. The setting was Thomas German Reed's bandbox Royal Gallery of Illustration ("gallery" being considered a more genteel name than "theatre" for a place that offered proper comic opera to prim Victorian audiences). There, *Ages Ago,* with music by Frederic Clay and words by W. S. Gilbert, was in rehearsal. Clay had invited his friend, composer Arthur Sullivan, to stop by, and so a high moment of theater history took place—although it went unmarked and unnoted—when he introduced the twenty-seven-year old musician to the thirty-three-year-old writer. The two men exchanged unremarkable pleasantries and went their separate ways, not to meet again until two years later, when they collaborated on their first opera, *Thespis.*

At the time of their first meeting, William Schwenck Gilbert was an established playwright as well as the author-illustrator of the "Bab Ballads" for the weekly journal *Fun,* and writer of drama criticism by the ream for whoever would publish it. He had taken a seventeen-year-old bride two years before: delicate, blonde, blue-eyed Agnes Turner, whom he called "Kitten" (and in a less romantic mood, "Missus"), the prototype of all the fair young women on whom he would have crushes during the years of a long and remarkably happy marriage.

Gilbert's childhood had been comfortable. His father, a naval surgeon with literary yearnings, once paid £25 to Neapolitan kidnappers for the return of his two-year-old "Bab." Years later Gilbert used the incident to advantage in *The Gondoliers,* where an infant prince is hidden away by his nurse and is later thought to have been left "gaily prattling with a highly respectable gondolier." Gilbert's childhood nickname surfaced later as well, affixed to his humorous ballads and illustrations in *Fun.*

Gilbert's earliest recorded attempt at light verse, written in an exercise book, was inspired when he was a schoolboy on vacation in Paris, recuperating from typhoid fever. He watched Napoleon III and

Three stars of the first Gilbert and Sullivan production of Iolanthe: *George Grossmith as the Lord Chancellor cavorts with Rutland Barrington's Earl of Mountararat, right, and Durward Lely's Earl Tolloller on the sheet-music cover.*

A Covent Garden Promenade Concert, pictured on a sheet-music cover of the time. Sullivan conducted some of his Pinafore *music in such a concert.*

Empress Eugénie ride past and, with his typically topsy-turvy point of view even then, wrote what the Emperor said upon seeing *him!*

And I never saw a phiz
More wonderful than 'is.

At school Gilbert earned some distinction for his translations of Greek and Latin verse, as well as acquiring a B.A. degree at King's College. Thus equipped to face the world, the young man went into the Civil Service, where he clerked for a niggardly £120 a year and tried to sell his clever verses on the side. As a volunteer in the 5th West Yorkshire Militia, he began his lifelong love affair with the uniforms and military accoutrements that would brighten many of his operas and enliven his personal wardrobe.

At last, after four lean years, a small legacy freed him to go into the law. He furnished a set of chambers in "a sombre little quadrangle" of Clement's Inn, attended theater and concerts when he could, and kept at his whimsical verses and drawings. Max Beerbohm, who loved the "Bab Ballads," later wrote of them:

> Literature has many a solemn masterpiece that one would without a qualm barter for that absurd and riotous one. Nor is the polished absurdity of the Savoy lyrics so dear as the riotous absurdity of those earlier ballads wherein you may find all the notions that informed the plots of the operas, together with a thousand and one other notions, and with a certain wild magic never quite recaptured.

In 1866 the London theater, if not opening its arms to the aspiring playwright, at least opened its stage door a crack when Gilbert was asked to write a parody of Donizetti's *L'Elisir d'Amore* for the Christmas burlesque at St. James's Theatre. *Dulcamara,* or *The Little Duck and The Great Quack* was Gilbert's maiden work for the theater, written in ten days, rehearsed for only a week, and, according to the then modest author, meeting with "more success than it deserved." In the flush of that success, inexperienced Gilbert asked for a fee of £30 for the play. Only after being paid was he advised by the manager, "Never sell so good a play as this for £30 again." He never did.

With one play to his credit, other commissions followed, though they were for the trashy ephemera that passed for musical theater at the time—burlesques and Christmas pantomimes. Nevertheless, these were a start and an opportunity for Gilbert to learn stagecraft. They also gave him a firmer financial underpinning than the law was able to afford, and at last the young man could think of marriage. Four months after his and Lucy's wedding, his *Harlequin Cock-Robin and Jenny Wren* was the Lyceum's 1867–68 pantomime.

In the following year, producer John Hollingshead opened the new Gaiety Theatre with Gilbert's parody of Giacomo Meyerbeer's *Robert le Diable.* The play was called *Robert the Devil,* or *The Nun, the Dun, and the Son of a Gun.* It was not much better than its title, but then what else on the London musical stage was, before Gilbert and Sullivan touched it with their combined genius?

John Hollingshead, who produced the first Gilbert and Sullivan opera, dropped the ball when he failed to continue the partnership.

Arthur Seymour Sullivan, on the day when he popped by the rehearsal at the Royal Gallery of Illustration, was a recently appointed professor at the Royal Academy of Music. For a young man of twenty-seven, born in the squalor of cockney Lambeth, he had already come a long way. At the age of twelve he was splendid in the scarlet and gold of the Chapel Royal choir; and sacred music and royal connections were to play a large part in his life forever after.

From his Italian mother and Irish bandmaster father, Sullivan received his warmth and charm and his musical gifts—his feeling for hauntingly romantic melody, for stirring church music, for the brisk and intricate rhythms of parade-ground tattoos. His musical genius announced itself at an early age, as did his radiant and amiable personality. "I shall miss your little happy face and black eyes at my dinner table," his mother wrote when he was thirteen and a chorister at the Chapel Royal.

Sullivan, in spite of the fragile health that plagued him all his life, accomplished a prodigious amount of composition. He had his first work—based on a verse from Hosea's lamentation "O Israel"—published when he was thirteen; he was the first winner of the Mendelssohn Scholarship to the Royal Academy of Music, which was twice renewed and included two further years of study at the Conservatorium in Leipzig that had been founded by that German composer. He was inspired to work hard. "I took lessons in counterpoint in the very room where Bach wrote all his works when in Leipzig," he later recalled, "so you can imagine the atmosphere of that room as being impregnated with counterpoint and fugue."

In Leipzig the handsome and personable young man found easy acceptance into society, and met Franz Liszt and Robert Schumann. At eighteen his composition *The Music to Shakespeare's Tempest* was performed in Leipzig and he wrote to his mother that it was "most successful. I was called forward three times afterwards"—a foreshadowing of his jubilant accounts of opening-night acclaim for each Gilbert and Sullivan opera in later years.

Young Sullivan returned to London hoping to be not only a composer but a conductor, an ambition that had inspired his comedian brother Fred (later to make his mark as the Judge in *Trial by Jury*) to write: ". . . you'll have no chance in London should you aspire to such a position for the market's overstocked with omnibuses."

But London in the 1860s was Sullivan's oyster. He composed concerti, piano works, his Symphony in E ("The Irish"), marches, overtures, an oratorio (*The Prodigal Son*), a ballet (*L'Ile Enchantée*), songs, religious music, and the two comic operas *Cox and Box* and *The Contrabandista,* the latter of which was commissioned in 1867 by Thomas German Reed, at whose theater Gilbert and Sullivan would first meet. Sullivan was soon taken up by Jenny Lind, the great singer, and her husband, Otto Goldschmidt. He visited Paris with Charles Dickens and George Grove and there met seventy-year-old Gioacchino Rossini, who was, he wrote in a memo, "composing a little pianoforte piece for his dog!" (Perhaps it was the delightful

Page of the manuscript score of Cox and Box, *Sullivan's first attempt at comic opera.*

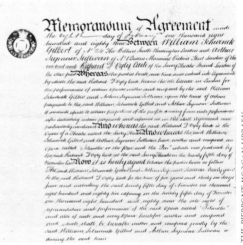

The first formal triumvirate contract signed by Gilbert, Sullivan, and D'Oyly Carte, in 1883, giving the impresario performance rights to Iolanthe *and subsequent operas for five years.*

The popularity of The Mikado *spawned countless commercial and merchandising byproducts well into the twentieth century.*

"poodle waltz" used many years later in Léonide Massine's Rossini ballet *La Boutique Fantasque*.) Indeed, the young Sullivan was, by his own admission, first inspired "with a love for the stage and things operatic" by the venerable composer of *The Barber of Seville*.

At the age of twenty-one Sullivan was commissioned to write no less than three of the special works, including the *Wedding March*, celebrating the shining event of the year: the marriage of the Prince of Wales (later Edward VII) to the beautiful Princess Alexandra of Denmark. It marked the beginning of the composer's relationship with the royal family. Over the years he became a member of the Prince of Wales's set, a close friend of the Duke of Edinburgh and the Princess Louise, and was knighted by their mother, Queen Victoria, at Windsor Castle in 1883—a good twenty-four years ahead of W. S. Gilbert.

Not until two years after their casual introduction were Gilbert and Sullivan brought together for a theatrical purpose. At that time Gilbert, the schoolboy translator of Greek and Latin verse, returned to his classical triumphs and wrote an "entirely original grotesque opera in two acts" about the gods on Mount Olympus. When impresario John Hollingshead sent the libretto of *Thespis*, or *The Gods Grown Old,* to Sullivan, the composer agreed, surprisingly, to write the score—embellished with such novel musical high jinks as train whistles and railway bells for Thespis's song about Diddlesex Junction.

The first joint effort of the men whose subsequent collaboration was Olympian turned out to be a flop—for reasons not solely due to the material itself. Yet four years later, under the banner of a thirty-

Impresario Richard D'Oyly Carte, dressed for the part, was caricatured brilliantly in 1891 by "Spy" (Leslie Ward) for Vanity Fair.

The new Savoy Theatre, pictured during the first act of Patience.

one-year-old impresario who was himself a musician and a man of taste, Gilbert and Sullivan came into their own as writers for the musical stage. With Richard D'Oyly Carte they made theatrical history in a partnership that began auspiciously in 1875 with *Trial by Jury,* scaled the heights with *H.M.S. Pinafore, The Pirates of Penzance,* and *The Mikado,* and not until twenty-one scintillating years later fizzled out with the final, disappointing production of *The Grand Duke.*

Where neither German Reed nor John Hollingshead had been able to profit from their earlier relationship and foster the successful union of Gilbert and Sullivan, young Carte, with exactly the necessary and unusual combination of perseverance, gifts, and abilities, struck sparks and forged the three-way partnership that was to revolutionize English comic opera.

Carte's family was musical and he himself had composed several operettas, had started a small theatrical agency, and in 1875 was managing the little Royalty Theatre in Soho, where a short Offenbach opera was failing to fill the till. Shrewdly, Carte thought to balance the French piece with an English curtain-raiser, and miraculously along came W. S. Gilbert, at thirty-nine an established and prosperous playwright (his 1871 *Pygmalion and Galatea* would earn him £40,000). Gilbert had recycled one of his "Bab Ballads," *Trial by Jury,* into a mock breach-of-promise lawsuit, its clever lyrics all to be set to music, with no spoken dialogue; the stately machinery of British justice was to be sent up in a mad and merry spoof that would mingle nonsense with sharpest mother wit. It was Carte who immediately thought to pair Sullivan's music with Gilbert's libretto, having the taste and acumen to see beyond the failure of *Thespis* to the potential strengths of the collaboration.

After the benchmark *Trial by Jury,* Carte was more tenacious than ever about his dream of "English comic opera in a theatre devoted to that alone." Harnessing his showmanship and taste to a group of men who could put up money but little else, he became managing director of the Comedy Opera Company. A theater was leased near the Strand; Gilbert and Sullivan were paid an advance on their next opera, *The Sorcerer*; but, most important of all, Carte ensured that the two creators were to be in complete control of their productions. Casting, costumes, sets, direction, rehearsals were their province and theirs alone. Inevitably, the financial backers grew greedy and litigation bankrupted the company, but, as a result, a simple new agreement drawn up by former barrister Gilbert in his own hand set up a new partnership in which the profits were equally shared by the three men.

While Gilbert and Sullivan created, Carte busied himself with American and foreign productions and an American tour that showered the men with fame and fortune beyond their dreams. Carte's own dream of an English musical theater was realized with the building of the Savoy Theatre in 1881, a marvel lighted by twelve hundred incandescent lamps instead of the old noxious gaslights. It gave its

THE PIERPONT MORGAN LIBRARY

This program for Patience *gives D'Oyly Carte top billing and uses the Savoy's innovative electric lights as a coat of arms.*

Arthur Sullivan, with monocle and baton, and W. S. Gilbert, the elegant Victorian clubman, as caricatured by "Spy" for Vanity Fair.

name to the D'Oyly Carte, Gilbert, and Sullivan company; they were known as the Savoyards, and thrived until 1982.

Today, Gilbert and Sullivan are reaching new and broader audiences than ever before, thanks to television productions that bring the irreverent lyrics and engaging melodies into twentieth-century living rooms. The partners' old magic is as potent now as it ever was, its sly laughter just below the surface:

> *We've a first-class assortment of magic;*
> *And for raising a posthumous shade*
> *With effects that are comic or tragic,*
> *There's no cheaper house in the trade.*
> *Love-philtre—we've quantities of it;*
> *And for knowledge if any one burns,*
> *We keep an extremely small prophet, a prophet*
> *Who brings us unbounded returns . . .*

John Wellington Wells's patter song from *The Sorcerer* still rings true.

The program cover by H. M. Brock for the 1920–21 D'Oyly Carte restaging of all the Gilbert and Sullivan operas illustrates the worldwide variety of their characters.

CHRONOLOGY OF THE OPERAS

COX AND BOX   1867

(Libretto by F. C. Burnand)
Benefit performance at Adelphi Theatre;
40 performances, Royal Gallery of Illustration

THESPIS   1871 (no longer played)
64 performances, Gaiety Theatre

TRIAL BY JURY   1875
131 performances, Royalty Theatre

THE SORCERER   1877
178 performances, Opéra Comique

H.M.S. PINAFORE   1878
571 performances, Opéra Comique

THE PIRATES OF PENZANCE   1879–80
One performance (for copyright), Royal Bijou Theater,
Paignton, Devon;
100 performances, Fifth Avenue Theater, New York;
363 performances, Opéra Comique

PATIENCE   1881
578 performances, Opéra Comique;
later opens Savoy Theatre

IOLANTHE   1882
398 performances, Savoy Theatre

PRINCESS IDA   1884
246 performances, Savoy Theatre

THE MIKADO   1885
672 performances, Savoy Theatre

RUDDIGORE   1887
288 performances, Savoy Theatre

THE YEOMEN OF THE GUARD   1888
423 performances, Savoy Theatre

THE GONDOLIERS   1889
554 performances, Savoy Theatre

UTOPIA LIMITED   1893
245 performances, Savoy Theatre (infrequently played)

THE GRAND DUKE   1896
123 performances, Savoy Theatre (infrequently played)

COX AND BOX

OR THE LONG-LOST BROTHERS

Although *Cox and Box* is regularly performed with the eleven Gilbert and Sullivan operas in the repertoire, it is really a cuckoo in the nest. Arthur Sullivan composed the music some three years before he met his destined librettist, and the book and lyrics for this short piece were written by F. C. Burnand, a humorist on the popular magazine *Punch,* who later became its editor.

The story goes that one day in 1866 Sullivan, then twenty-four years old and already a successful composer of serious music, chanced upon Burnand in Bond Street. The writer was delighted at the encounter—he was looking for a musical entertainment to put on at a private party and he suggested that Sullivan might provide the music for a little one-act farce called *Box and Cox,* for which he would supply the libretto. It was just the excuse Sullivan needed to try his hand at a bit of frivolous, light music. Burlesque was all the rage in Paris and London, and if this piece was to be performed at a private party, it could not possibly harm his professional reputation as a serious composer.

The play *Box and Cox,* about a dishonest lodging-house keeper and her two tenants, became the opera *Cox and Box,* while the lodging-house keeper, *Mrs.* Bouncer, was turned into a landlord, *Sergeant* Bouncer. Sullivan dashed off the music quickly, and the private performance was put on at Moray Lodge, the Kensington residence of Arthur Lewis and his actress wife Kate Terry for a party of theatrical folk. (The Lewises' grandson is the illustrious theatrical knight Sir John Gielgud.)

So well received was this private entertainment that a year later it was performed in public for a benefit at the Adelphi Theatre with Sullivan playing the piano accompaniment and Burnand's colleague on *Punch,* the artist George du Maurier, playing Box. Later in his life the versatile du Maurier was to achieve a second fame as the author of *Trilby* and *Peter Ibbetson.*

A Victorian London slum, with pinched face children, is the unlikely setting for the farcical shenanigans of two lodgers and their crooked landlord.

Neighborhood characters serenade outside Sergeant Bouncer's lodging house.

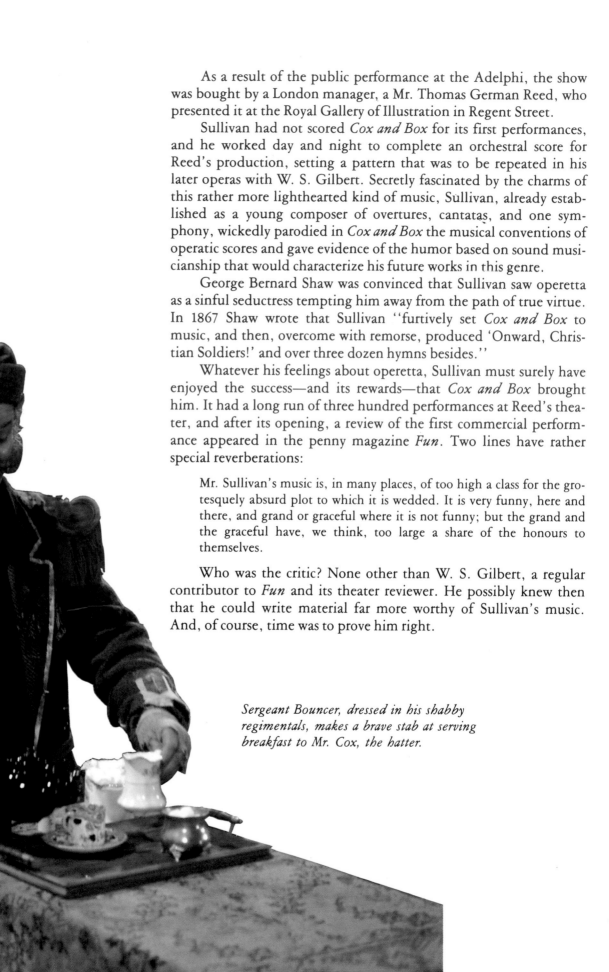

As a result of the public performance at the Adelphi, the show was bought by a London manager, a Mr. Thomas German Reed, who presented it at the Royal Gallery of Illustration in Regent Street.

Sullivan had not scored *Cox and Box* for its first performances, and he worked day and night to complete an orchestral score for Reed's production, setting a pattern that was to be repeated in his later operas with W. S. Gilbert. Secretly fascinated by the charms of this rather more lighthearted kind of music, Sullivan, already established as a young composer of overtures, cantatas, and one symphony, wickedly parodied in *Cox and Box* the musical conventions of operatic scores and gave evidence of the humor based on sound musicianship that would characterize his future works in this genre.

George Bernard Shaw was convinced that Sullivan saw operetta as a sinful seductress tempting him away from the path of true virtue. In 1867 Shaw wrote that Sullivan "furtively set *Cox and Box* to music, and then, overcome with remorse, produced 'Onward, Christian Soldiers!' and over three dozen hymns besides."

Whatever his feelings about operetta, Sullivan must surely have enjoyed the success—and its rewards—that *Cox and Box* brought him. It had a long run of three hundred performances at Reed's theater, and after its opening, a review of the first commercial performance appeared in the penny magazine *Fun*. Two lines have rather special reverberations:

> Mr. Sullivan's music is, in many places, of too high a class for the grotesquely absurd plot to which it is wedded. It is very funny, here and there, and grand or graceful where it is not funny; but the grand and the graceful have, we think, too large a share of the honours to themselves.

Who was the critic? None other than W. S. Gilbert, a regular contributor to *Fun* and its theater reviewer. He possibly knew then that he could write material far more worthy of Sullivan's music. And, of course, time was to prove him right.

Sergeant Bouncer, dressed in his shabby regimentals, makes a brave stab at serving breakfast to Mr. Cox, the hatter.

Cox and Box discover to their fury that their landlord has rented them both the same room. "Bouncer!" they shout. "Turn out the man!"

COX AND BOX

OR THE LONG-LOST BROTHERS

SCENE: *A room; a bed, with curtains closed; three doors; a window; a fireplace; table and chairs.*

IN A SEEDY NEIGHBORHOOD OF VICTORIAN LONDON there is a run-down lodging house operated by one Sergeant Bouncer, an erstwhile military man in Her Majesty's forces. Several other old soldiers scrounge for a living on the street, their tattered regimental great-coats offering some small protection against the penetrating fog. Derelicts and pinched-face urchins, blowzy women, a fruit and vegetable vendor, a barmaid on her way to work, and a decrepit hansom cab can be glimpsed through the wisps of fog.

The lodging house, with its peeling wallpaper and depressingly brown woodwork, at least offers some shelter from the wretched world beyond its front door. As a matter of fact, the squalid room of one of its lodgers is, this very morning, a scene of comparative luxury. In the center of the room stands a tin hip bath afoam with soapsuds. Above the white froth protrudes the head of a young man, James John Cox. Sergeant Bouncer, wielding a straight razor with the brio of an accomplished swordsman, is shaving the young man's lathered face.

"Why, you've had your hair cut!" the Sergeant exclaims.

"Cut!" Cox shouts. "It strikes me I've had it mowed! I look as if I'd been cropped for the Army—"

"The Army!" Bouncer interrupts, eager to divert Cox from his displeasure. "I recollect when I was in the Militia . . . ." And he launches into a spirited rataplan drum song, his customary dodge for changing the subject when tempers threaten to explode.

Dramatis Personae:

JAMES JOHN COX, a Journeyman Hatter (Baritone)

JOHN JAMES BOX, a Journeyman Printer (Tenor)

SERGEANT BOUNCER, a Lodging-house Keeper, with Military Reminiscences (Baritone)

First public performance at the Adelphi Theatre, May 11, 1867.

The roguish Sergeant enjoys an unmilitary encounter on the stairs.

Before going off to work, Cox demands a word with a frightened Bouncer, whose conduct he has begun to suspect.

Bouncer hurriedly prepares the room for Box the printer, whom he sees approaching the house.

Marching about the room while Cox is getting dressed, Bouncer distracts the lodger with his martial drumbeat song:

We sounded the trumpet, we beat the drum,
Somehow the enemy didn't come,
*   So I gave up my horse*
*   In Her Majesty's force. . . .*

*   There wasn't a man*
*   In the rear or the van,*
Who found an occasion to sing Rataplan!
Rataplan! Rataplan! Rataplan! Rataplan, plan, plan, plan!

By song's end Cox is dressed, his ill humor over the haircut quite dissipated. But there has been a more serious matter troubling him, and here the plot of this little comic opera begins to thicken.

Cox asks his landlord, ever so casually, how it is that when he comes home at night he frequently finds his apartment full of smoke; the landlord lamely supposes it's the chimney.

"The chimney doesn't smoke tobacco," Cox snaps. "I'm speaking of tobacco smoke."

Bouncer replies that the gentleman "who has got the attics" smokes a pipe and Cox guesses that that must be the individual he invariably meets coming up the stairs when he is going down, and going down when he is coming up. Bouncer stammers an answer and tries to beat a swift retreat.

It is clear that the landlord is something of a crook. He has managed to earn twice as much rent from his room by the artful dodge of letting it to two tenants at once: Cox, a hatter, who works days, and Box, a printer, who works nights. And so, when Cox calls him back "to have a word," Bouncer cringes and sings in an aside, "I tremble—ah! I tremble!"

The irate tenant complains about his mysteriously dwindling supplies:

Now, coals is coals, as sure as eggs is eggs,
Coals haven't souls, no more than they have legs;
But, as you will admit, the case is so,
Legs or no legs, my coals contrive to go!

Bouncer manages to calm the angry young man's suspicions and gets him off to work to the distracting tune of a military rataplan. The landlord then scurries about the room, putting Mr. Cox's things out of Mr. Box's sight—just in the nick of time. We hear Box's voice beyond the door shouting, "Why don't you keep your own side of the staircase, sir?"

As the printer stamps into the room, tired and ill-tempered from a long night of setting type, the landlord sidles out the door only to be called back sharply. Box wants to know about the man he encounters every day, going downstairs when he is coming up, and coming upstairs when he is going down, wearing such a variety of hats that he must be "associated with the hatting interest."

The ingenious Bouncer tells him that the gentleman with the hats lives in the attic, and adds triumphantly: ". . . that's why he took the *hattics!*" While Box—and the audience—are thinking that one over, the wily Bouncer slips out the door.

The room has been somewhat rearranged to suit this tenant— the bed made up, the hip bath removed—and Box, contented to be at home, neatly lays out a package of bacon and a penny roll. He is looking forward to a good breakfast before his sleep. A careful man, he is annoyed to find that Sergeant Bouncer has apparently used all but one of his matches. Grumbling all the while, he lights the fire with his last match, puts the pan with his rasher of bacon on the fire, and sings a little lullaby that starts, "Hushed is the bacon on the

Among the little luxuries provided by the Sergeant is a sudsy hip bath for the fastidious hatter.

grid.'' Box's sweet tenor, the 4/4 time, and the soothing *andante* tempo work their magic. Box's head nods, and he toddles off, midsong, to the curtained bed, where he falls asleep instantly.

No sooner has Box disappeared behind his bed curtains than a jaunty Cox dances into the room. He has been given an unexpected day off and has come home ''for my breakfast, my light *de-jeu-nay*,'' for which he has supplied himself with a handsome mutton chop.

But what's this! The fire is lighted, and there on his gridiron a rasher of bacon is sputtering away. ''Well, now,'' Cox exclaims, '' 'pon my life, there is a quiet coolness about Bouncer's proceedings that's almost amusing. He takes my last lucifer—my coals—and my gridiron, to cook his breakfast by! No, no—I can't stand this!'' and he removes the bacon to a plate, replacing it on the gridiron with his

The weary printer takes possession of his room and bed, singing, ''I'll take a nap and close my eye . . .''

chop. "Now then, for my things," he says with some satisfaction and goes out to the left, slamming the door behind him.

"Come in!" Box calls sleepily from behind the bed curtains, awakened by the slam. Suddenly he bounds out of bed, worried that his bacon has burned while he slept, and is furious to see a chop— "Whose chop? Bouncer's"—on the fire in its place. "Well, 'pon my life! And shall I curb my indignation?" he asks himself rhetorically. "No!" he shouts, spearing the offending chop with his fork and throwing it out the window. Then he puts his bacon back on the gridiron and goes out the door at the right to get his breakfast things, slamming the door behind him.

"Come in—come in!" Cox calls, opening the door to the left and carrying in a tray set with his tea things. Remembering his chop, he runs to the fireplace only to find the bacon again. "Confound it— dash it—damn it," he swears. "I can't stand this!" And he pokes his fork into the bacon and flings it out the window.

Returning to the fireplace for his tea tray, he encounters Box, in nightshirt and robe, carrying *his* tray.

"Who are you, sir? tell me who?" asks Cox in his baritone.

"If it comes to that, sir, who are you?" Box's tenor answers, and they are off, in a tempo that eventually quickens to an *allegro furioso.*

"What's that to you, sir?"

"What's that to *who*, sir?"

"Who, sir? You, sir?"

The two lodgers sing an angry duet:

*Printer, printer, take a hin*ter,
Hatter, hatter, cease your clatter

during the course of which each shows the other a rent receipt for the room, and they shout for Bouncer to settle the matter and convert the duet to a trio. "Thieves!" "Murder!" "Bouncer! . . . Turn out the man!"

The Sergeant marches in with all the neighborhood characters in tow, singing briskly to distract his angry tenants: "Rataplan, Rataplan, Rataplan, Rataplan!" and the ploy works—momentarily. The angry lodgers join in with a lusty, "Rataplan, plan, plan, plan!" as the whole troupe stomps about the room. But Box and Cox soon return to the issue and demand an explanation from their landlord.

In his most ingratiating manner that scamp says, "Gents, don't be angry—but, you see, this gentleman [pointing to Box] only being at home in the daytime, and that gentleman [pointing to Cox] at night, I thought I might venture, until my little back second floor room was ready . . . ."

When Cox and Box learn that the second-floor room will be ready tomorrow, they both say they'll take it. To which Bouncer sensibly points out, "Excuse me—but if you both take it, you may just as well stop where you are."

Cox has been given an unexpected holiday, and while Box snoozes behind his bed curtain Cox sings, "Now for my breakfast, my light de-jeu-nay."

The jig is up when Cox and Box discover each other and join in a furious duet about their "raging fierce desire" to do each other an injury!

"True," they answer. They then fall to arguing about which of them should go out for a bit of exercise, and which (Box, remember, has missed his day's sleep) shall retire to his pillow.

". . . my bed."

"*Your* bed?"

After halfheartedly threatening to fight or to call the police, both agree that they have no violent animosity, no rooted antipathy to one another, and it is Bouncer who is at fault. They may as well wait patiently for the little back room to be ready.

Cox dabbles in a serenade:
"The buttercup dwells on the lowly mead,
  The daisy is bright to see;
But brighter far are the eyes that read
  The thoughts in the heart of me."

Meanwhile, to pass the time, Box asks Cox if he sings.

"I sometimes dabble in a serenade," the hatter admits modestly.

"Then dabble away," says the printer. Cox takes up a guitar, on which he strums an accompaniment to their duet serenade, "The Buttercup." Box, in his cadenza, "I play on the concertina . . ." hits a high B-flat that probably earns him the admiration of Cox as well as of the audience.

After this interval of vocal harmony the two men find themselves in general accord and exchange friendly confidences. Cox, who seems less than happy about his circumstances, admits that he has an intended wife, the proprietor of a considerable number of bathing machines at the seaside resort of Margate. "In the bathing season—which, luckily, is rather a long one—we see but little of each other."

Box says he's not exactly married, not precisely a happy bachelor, not absolutely a widower, and in answer to Cox's wondering how he—or any man alive—could help but be one of the three, replies: ". . . but I'm not alive!"

Naturally, Cox is incredulous.

"If you won't believe me, I'll refer you to a very large, numerous, and respectable circle of disconsolate friends," the printer tells him.

Cox, with a gleam of hope in his eye, grasps Box's arm. "My dear sir—my *very* dear sir—if there does exist any ingenious contrivance whereby a man on the eve of committing matrimony can leave this world, and yet stop in it, I shouldn't be sorry to know it."

He is somewhat relieved to hear from Box that there is nothing easier, if he just does as the printer did.

"I will! What is it?"

"Drown yourself!" the printer tells him simply. But then Box explains in a mock-romantic ballad:

Not long ago it was my fate to captivate a widow,
At Ramsgate.

Cox confides that

I, 'tis odd to state, the same at Margate did, oh!

Box continues his story of the widow's persistent courtship, with Cox hanging on his every word.

The happy day came near at length—
We hoped it would be sunny;
I found I needed all my strength
To face the ceremony.

And then, Box relates, he suddenly realized he was unworthy to possess the lady. His modest reluctance resulted in a domestic tempest of "Clattering, spattering, battering, shattering,/Dashing, clashing, smashing, flashing, slashing, crashing—missing . . ." crockery and slop basins.

Before this harmony is achieved, the Sergeant has created a diversion by marching in with the neighborhood characters, all singing a lusty "Rataplan, Rataplan, Rataplan, Rataplan!"

"O ciel!" breathes Cox, "proceed."

Box, walking out on the little balcony overlooking the street, describes, in mock-operatic style, how one morning he packed up his bundle and off he went, walked to the edge of the cliff, saw that no one was there, looked down at the sea, cried farewell to the earth, to the land of his birth, to his only love, to the sea and the sky, lay down his bundle where the coast guard was sure to pass—and walked away in the opposite direction.

Cox hears this recital with mounting admiration and resolves to try Box's wonderful contrivance himself. "What a clever man! What a capital plan! . . . Ingenious creature! you disappeared—the suit of clothes was found—"

Box accepts the praise as his just due, but adds the detail that he considers the crowning artistic touch to his brilliant fabrication a piece of paper found in the coat pocket with these affecting farewell words: "This is thy work, oh, Penelope Ann!"

Cox is stunned. "Penelope Ann! Penelope Ann?" he exclaims.

And, of course, it is the same matrimonially inclined bathing machine proprietor of Margate from whose toils he himself is trying to slip. But now there is a better way out. He seizes Box and vows not to lose sight of him until he has restored him to the interesting creature he has so cruelly deceived. "I give her up to you."

But Box will have none of it, claiming that, as he is drowned, he cannot have her. An argument ensues and with much violent ringing of bells and calls for Bouncer the two lodgers, ready to duel to the death, demand: "Pistols for two!" While the landlord is fetching the pistols (mercifully unloaded, or Box and Cox wouldn't have touched them) they admit to each other that they can't abide Penelope Ann, and would never be happy with her.

When Bouncer returns, he apologizes for not being able to find the pistols but he does have a letter he forgot to deliver to Mr. Cox since yesterday. Cox looks at the letter. " 'Margate,' " he reads. "Penelope Ann!"

The landlord edges out of the room before he can be scolded for his negligence. But Box and Cox are much too absorbed in the message to care.

" 'Dear Mr. Cox,' " reads Box. " 'Pardon my candor' "—

" 'But being convinced that our feelings, like our ages, do not reciprocate' "—continues Cox.

" 'I hasten to apprise you of my immediate union' "—Box reads on.

" 'With Mr. Knox,' " Cox finishes triumphantly.

The two lodgers send up three cheers for Knox and rush downstairs to the corner pub to celebrate their double escape.

When Bouncer comes there looking for his lodgers to give them the good news that the little second-floor back room is quite ready, the two former enemies astonish him.

"I don't want it," says Cox.

The brothers will now share their room, their lives—and even their umbrella.

The corner pub is the scene of the long-lost brothers' reunion . . . and of a final rousing "Rataplan!" with landlord Bouncer.

"No more do I!" Box adds.

Deciding that nothing will ever come between them, Cox and Box are about to embrace when Box, looking intently at Cox's face, says, "You'll excuse the apparent insanity of the remark, but the more I gaze on your features, the more I'm convinced that you're my long-lost brother."

Cox admits he's had the same thought.

"Tell me," says Box, ". . . have you such a thing as a strawberry mark on your left arm?"

"No!" Cox answers.

"Then it is he!"

And so saying, the brothers rush into each other's arms.

Joined by Bouncer and the neighborhood characters, all march about the pub singing a final rousing rataplan:

My hand upon it, join but yours; agree the house will hold us.
And two good lodgers Bouncer gets, he'll in his arms enfold us.
Rataplan, Rataplan, plan, plan, plan, plan . . .

Yes—Rataplan—Penelope Ann
Has married another respectable man. . . .

TRIAL BY JURY

On the night of March 25, 1875, an event of far-reaching theatrical importance took place at the Royalty Theatre, though at the time no one could have realized it. A modest little curtain-raiser billed as a "dramatic cantata" made its debut to fill out the evening with Offenbach's *La Périchole*, which ran a bit short. It was the first collaboration of producer Richard D'Oyly Carte, librettist William Schwenck Gilbert, and composer Arthur Seymour Sullivan.

Gilbert and Sullivan had written an ill-fated short opera, *Thespis*, or *The Gods Grown Old*, some four years earlier as an afterpiece for one of producer John Hollingsworth's burlesques. This first operatic collaboration failed and the two men shook hands and went their separate ways again, Gilbert returning to his successful writing of comedies, Sullivan to his composing and conducting triumphs with serious music. Nearly all the music of *Thespis*, never published, has been lost. *Thespis* has never been played again.

D'Oyly Carte, a thirty-one-year-old theater manager with sound musical background, a keen business sense, and cultivated taste, had a dream: "The starting of English comic opera in a theatre devoted to that alone was the scheme of my life." Early in 1875 the dream seemed far from fulfillment. Box office receipts at the Royalty were down, possibly because the Offenbach offering was too slight, and the manager had been considering the addition of a curtain-raiser in the lighthearted vein of the popular French composer, but with an English flavor.

It was at that moment that fate, in the guise of Mr. W. S. Gilbert, knocked at the door. Carte welcomed the playwright and mentioned his need for a short, humorous opener and by great good luck Gilbert just happened to have the completed libretto of a breach of contract piece, *Trial by Jury*. It was an expanded version of a one-page "Bab Ballad" he had written and illustrated for *Fun* magazine five years earlier, and he hoped Carl Rosa, the opera manager, would write the music for the one-act cantata.

The opening night of Thespis *disastrously introduced the highbrow gods of Mount Olympus to the burlesque stage of the Gaiety.*

"And now, if you please, I'm ready to try/This Breach of Promise of Marriage!"

Carte read the piece and liked it. The script was witty and full of jokes about the legal profession—Gilbert had trained as a barrister himself but had abandoned the law for the theater. Carte now showed his mettle as an impresario. Remembering the positive promise of the failed *Thespis* (whose Chairman of the North South East West Diddlesex Junction Railway was "conspicuous exceeding/ For his happy way and easy breeding," and whose song was amusingly punctuated by a locomotive bell and whistle), he proposed that Sullivan and no other collaborate once again with Gilbert. The playwright demurred, but Carte overruled him, so convinced was he that Gilbert and Sullivan had the makings of a unique combination.

Angelina, the jilted Plaintiff, enjoys a hearty breakfast in bed before her appearance in court.

He urged Gilbert to bring his script to the composer, and the author finally agreed. There in Sullivan's rooms, before a blazing fire, "he read it through to me in a perturbed sort of way with a gradual crescendo of indignation, in the manner of a man considerably disappointed with what he had written," Sullivan recalled. "As soon as he had come to the last word he closed up the manuscript violently, apparently unconscious of the fact that he had achieved his purpose so far as I was concerned—I was screaming with laughter the whole time."

Within the short space of three weeks, the music was written and rehearsals were completed. D'Oyly Carte advertised the work, with true showman's panache, as "a novel and entirely original dramatic cantata." The star of the show was Fred Sullivan, Arthur's talented brother, who delighted audiences in the role of the Learned Judge, a good-humored old reprobate who was highly susceptible to the charms of the young plaintiff and her pretty bridesmaids. On opening night the composer himself conducted the orchestra.

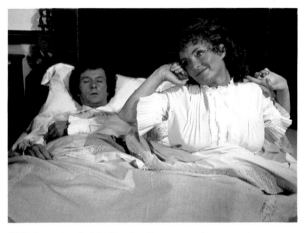

Edwin, the fickle Defendant, awakens with his new love, while Angelina and her bridesmaids prepare to dazzle the Judge and the Jury.

The little masterpiece of purely musical storytelling—there is no spoken dialogue—was an immediate success. Audiences and reviewers loved it, with *Punch*'s critic, exposed to the best humorists of the time, writing, "In *Trial by Jury* both Mr. Words and Mr. Music have worked together and for the first quarter of an hour the Cantata (as they have called it) is the funniest bit of nonsense your representative has seen for a considerable time."

The English curtain-raiser for *La Périchole* outlasted the Offenbach opera and continued to be the draw when it was teamed with Lecocq's *La Fille de Madame Angot*. In three London theaters from 1875 to 1877 it played for two hundred performances, its run ending only with the untimely death of its star, Fred Sullivan. It was a success that augured well for D'Oyly Carte's dream of English comic opera. The collaboration that was born with *Trial by Jury* produced a dozen more comic operas, all but two of them still performed today.

TRIAL BY JURY

SCENE: *A court of justice. Barristers, Attorneys, and Jurymen discovered.*

IN THE AUSTERE COURT OF THE EXCHEQUER, where a breach of promise case is about to be tried, the full majesty of the English judiciary is on display. The wood-paneled courtroom; the Bench with its throne-like chair from which the Learned Judge will preside beneath the royal coat of arms; the barristers, "be-wigged and be-gowned," all create a setting that is authentic and awe-inspiring.

We are reminded that William Gilbert at one time had himself practiced law at Clerkenwell Sessions House, on which the original stage set was modeled, and knew whereof he wrote. He has given us a Learned Judge, a Jury, a Plaintiff and Defendant, a Counsel, and an Usher, all of whom, in deference to the setting, perform with complete seriousness. But wait a bit. Before very long these characters manage to skew the action in such a way that we are laughing (as Arthur Sullivan had) at justice run amok in this outrageous lampoon.

The curtain rises on a proper courtroom where immediately a chorus of jurymen, barristers, and attorneys lets us know what to expect:

> *Hark, the hour of ten is sounding:*
> *Hearts with anxious fears are bounding,*
> *Hall of Justice crowds surrounding,*
> *   Breathing hope and fear—*
> *For to-day in this arena,*
> *Summoned by a stern subpoena,*
> *Edwin, sued by Angelina,*
> *   Shortly will appear.*

The Usher, punctual and punctilious, makes his entrance on the last stroke of ten, robed in black and carrying his tall mace topped with a golden crown. He sternly advises the jurymen to set aside all vulgar prejudice, because

Dramatis Personae:

THE LEARNED JUDGE (Baritone)

THE PLAINTIFF, Angelina (Soprano)

THE DEFENDANT, Edwin (Tenor)

COUNSEL FOR THE PLAINTIFF (Baritone)

USHER (Bass)

FOREMAN OF THE JURY (Bass)

ASSOCIATE

FIRST BRIDESMAID

Chorus of Barristers, Attorneys, Jurymen, Bridesmaids

First produced at the Royalty Theatre, March 25, 1875.

"See my interesting client, / Victim of a heartless wile!"

From bias free of every kind,
This trial must be tried.

As the chorus dutifully repeats the last two lines, the Usher blasts out a fortissimo "Silence in Court!" over their voices, waving his staff wildly. We begin to see the joke. He then launches into a thoroughly biased description of the Plaintiff, "the broken-hearted bride," to whom they must listen, and the "ruffianly Defendant," whose testimony they needn't mind, while repeating his mealy-mouthed appeal to fairness several times. It is obvious that we are in topsy-turvy land where many a truth will be said in jest.

Meanwhile the composer, too, is having his fun. The bell-like sounds when the chorus sings "Hark, the hour of ten is sounding" would have tickled Victorian audiences recognizing in Sullivan's parody the monks' bells in Lecocq's popular *La Poupée (The Doll)*.

Just when the stage has been set for the kind of justice the Defendant is likely to receive, the young man diffidently enters and asks if this is the Court of the Exchequer. Told that it is, Edwin prepares himself to be firm, though his evil star is in the ascendant.

And indeed, the jurymen, upon learning that this is the Defendant, shake their fists at him while singing:

Monster, dread our damages.
We're the jury,
Dread our fury!

But Edwin is not abashed. Bravely he points out that these are very strange proceedings, since the jury is quite in the dark about the merits of his pleadings and should hear him out. He beckons to the jurymen, who leave the box and gather round while he sings them an eighteen-line ditty that is possibly the most pragmatic love song ever written:

When my first old, old love I knew,
My bosom welled with joy;
My riches at her feet I threw—
I was a love-sick boy!
No terms seemed too extravagant
Upon her to employ—
I used to mope, and sigh, and pant,
Just like a love-sick boy.
Tink-a-Tank—Tink-a-Tank.

But joy incessant palls the sense;
And love, unchanged, will cloy,
And she became a bore intense
Unto her love-sick boy!
With fitful glimmer burnt my flame,
And I grew cold and coy,
At last, one morning, I became
Another's love-sick boy.
Tink-a-Tank—Tink-a-Tank.

"Now, Jurymen, hear my advice—
All kinds of vulgar prejudice
I pray you set aside:
With stern judicial frame of mind . . .
This trial must be tried."

The jurymen, of course, cannot fail to empathize with Edwin's frank account of how it is when love grows cold. They admit that, to a man, they were just like that "when a boy," shocking young scamps, rovers, regular cads. *But*—now that all that is over and they are respectable chaps, and shining with virtue resplendent— why, they haven't a scrap of sympathy for the defendant.

"Consider the moral, I pray,
  Nor bring a young fellow to sorrow,
Who loves this young lady to-day,
  And loves that young lady to-morrow."

And they return to the jury-box, "Singing so merrily—Trial-la-Law!/Trial-la-Law—Trial-la-Law!/Singing so merrily—Trial-la-Law!" Things are looking bleak for the poor Defendant, but there is still the Learned Judge to be reckoned with, the embodiment of British justice, who should give Edwin a fair shake at last.

Indeed, the Judge's entrance is impressive, with the Usher demanding silence in court and that all present "in due submission bend," while the full chorus sings a Handelian "all hail" to his bright rays, and vows that they will "never grudge ecstatic praise." The audience, of course, was as entranced with Sullivan's deft spoofs of serious music as with Gilbert's clever put-downs of the country's most respected institutions. The *Times* critic noted that "No situation has been overlooked in which the music can be made comically subservient to the dramatic import . . . it seems, as in the great Wagnerian operas, as though poem and music had proceeded simultaneously from one and the same brain."

The Learned Judge is the first in the long line of Gilbert's witty characterizations whose tongue-tripping patter songs reveal their all-too-human frailties. Fred Sullivan, Arthur's brother, created the role (with "valuable suggestions" from the playwright), and although he was the hit of the show, one member of the audience, the Lord Chief Justice, objected to the portrait, testily declaring it "calculated to bring the bench into contempt," and he refused to attend again "for fear he should seem to encourage it."

The Learned Judge is an engaging old scamp, who, in spite of yards of red velvet and ermine and a magnificent wig, still looks slightly disreputable. As he settles himself in his high seat of honor, he glosses over the business of the day—"A Breach of Promise"—in order first to tell the Court how he came to be a judge.

His is a plain, unvarnished tale, with no apologies, of a young barrister, an "impecunious party," who owned a blue swallow-tail coat, a couple of shirts and collars, "and a ring that looked like a ruby!" He was beginning to grow semi-despondent about his chances of ever addressing a British jury, and

> . . . I soon got tired of third-class journeys,
>   And dinners of bread and water;
> So I fell in love with a rich attorney's
>   Elderly, ugly daughter.

The rich attorney was overjoyed and promised the young barrister that he'd reap his reward by being the recipient of all the briefs he could throw his way for cases at the important courts. He further backed up the young man's wavering resolution:

The bevy of beribboned Victorian brides-maids trip through the courtroom, sweeping Justice and the Law before them.

> "You'll soon get used to her looks," said he,
>   "And a very nice girl you'll find her!
> She may very well pass for forty-three
>   In the dusk, with a light behind her!"

As the favored son-in-law, the barrister enjoyed, as guaranteed, a busy and lucrative practice:

All thieves who could my fees afford
  Relied on my orations,
And many a burglar I've restored
  To his friends and his relations.

But eventually—and here the Judge's recital echoes Edwin's candid fickleness—the story takes a familiar turn:

At length I became as rich as the Gurneys—
  An incubus then I thought her,
So I threw over that rich attorney's
  Elderly, ugly daughter.
The rich attorney my character high
  Tried vainly to disparage—
And now, if you please, I'm ready to try
  This Breach of Promise of Marriage!

The Foreman of the Jury and Angelina's skillful Counsel comfort the fainting Plaintiff.

One has the impression that the Learned Judge, like the Defendant, will one fine morning find himself another love. Nevertheless, who can resist the delicious impudence of such a man judging a breach of promise case?

And now the stage is set for the trial to begin. Counsel asks for the Plaintiff to be brought in, and the Usher sings out Angelina's name, first to one side of the courtroom, where an echo sings it back, then to the other side, an octave lower, where again it is echoed. But the echo cannot reach the lowest note of the last syllable, and the Usher, with a smug smile, finishes Angelina's name for him—a typical bit of playful Gilbert and Sullivan business that has endeared them to audiences for the past hundred years.

At this point, the staid courtroom is invaded by a bevy of entrancing young bridesmaids in high-laced kid boots, flounced Victorian gowns, and carrying beribboned nosegays. All the men, except the Defendant, perk up as the sweet voices sing a song that begins: "Comes the broken flower—/Comes the cheated maid—" The bridesmaids continue their sad song as they make their progress around the courtroom, not without good effect. The Judge in great excitement sends the Usher with a note to the First Bridesmaid, who reads it, kisses it rapturously, and tucks it in her bosom.

The Learned Judge, who has never seen "so exquisitely fair a face," listens sympathetically to Angelina's Counsel and will offer his own shoulder to the weeping bride.

But at that moment the lovely Angelina, in her virginal bridal finery, enters and the Judge is instantly smitten:

Oh, never, never, never, since I joined the human race,
Saw I so exquisitely fair a face.

His admiration is swiftly transferred from Bridesmaid to jilted Bride, and just as swiftly the Usher takes the billet-doux from the former and delivers it to the latter. Angelina reads it, kisses it rapturously, and tucks it in *her* bosom.

Her Counsel now addresses the Judge and the jury, pulling out all the stops in "this painful case," while Angelina falls sobbing on his breast. He describes his client as the victim of a heartless wile, tells how she smiled sweetly at the traitorous Defendant, wooed and won him, finally named—and insisted on—the day. He has everyone in the courtroom hanging on every word as he scowls at Edwin.

Picture him excuses framing—
Going from her far away;
Doubly criminal to do so,
For the maid has bought her trousseau!

Angelina's sobs increase at this final, most costly, perfidy and she seems about to faint. The jury is moved to call out comfortingly that they love her; the Foreman invites her to lean on him and tells her he'd enjoy being just like a father to her. The Judge leaps up and offers his shoulder instead for her to recline on. And, of course, Angelina recovers enough to jump onto the Bench, sit down next to the Learned Judge, and fall sobbing on *his* breast.

The jury, thoroughly aroused, shake fists at the Defendant and chant:

Edwin sings his defense:
"Though I own that my heart has been ranging,
Of nature the laws I obey,
For nature is constantly changing."

Monster, monster, dread our fury—
There's the Judge, and we're the Jury!
Come! Substantial damages,
Dam—

They are cut short by the Usher's loud demand for silence, leaving a most un-Victorian oath hanging on the air, an example of Gilbert's words and Sullivan's music combining for a slyly mischievous effect. And the silence permits the Defendant finally to speak out in his defense.

Edwin makes an eloquent plea for inconstancy—he obeys the laws of nature, he explains, and everyone knows nature is "constantly changing." There are the phases of the moon, the time, wind, and weather, the months and days ("And you don't find two Mondays together"):

Consider the moral, I pray,
  Nor bring a young fellow to sorrow,
Who loves this young lady to-day,
  And loves that young lady to-morrow. . . .

And it's not in the range of belief,
  To look upon him as a glutton,
Who, when he is tired of beef,
  Determines to tackle the mutton.

Edwin then proposes a very practical solution to Angelina's charges:

  If it will appease her sorrow,
I'll marry this lady to-day,
  And I'll marry the other to-morrow!

The Learned Judge, eager to have his work at an end, is quick to say that this seems to him a reasonable proposition, but Counsel, referring to his lawbook, demurs, saying that to marry two at once is, plain and simple, "Burglaree," and that in the reign of James the Second it was considered a very great crime. At which the entire Court sighs in admiration, "Oh, man of learning!"

The Judge, Counsel, Defendant, and Plaintiff now engage in a charming little quartet in which they describe the "nice dilemma we have here" that will call for "all our wit." If Edwin is loath to marry the girl, he will have committed a breach; and if he marries Angelina as well as his present love, it will count as Burglaree! A nice dilemma indeed.

Angelina decides to take matters into her own firm little hands and, slipping down from the Judge's side, she joins Edwin and folds him in a rapturous embrace.

I love him—I love him—with fervour unceasing
  I worship and madly adore. . . .

Oh, see what a blessing, what love and caressing
  I've lost, and remember it, pray,
When you I'm addressing, are busy assessing
  The damages Edwin must pay!

Angelina's Counsel firmly rejects Edwin's offer to wed both young ladies: "To marry two at once is Burglaree!"

The Defendant repels his would-be bride furiously, and having extricated himself from her unsolicited embrace he now tries to free himself from her unwanted ardor by cataloging all his vices. He tells her—and the Court—that he smokes like a chimney, he drinks, he's a ruffian and a bully; he paints a lurid picture of how, when in his cups, he's sure he would beat her and kick her; and finally he suggests that Angelina wouldn't be able to endure him even for a day. He begs the Court to consider all of this when they assess the damages he should pay.

But Angelina clings to the Defendant passionately and at last, after a struggle, he manages to throw her off into the eager arms of her Counsel.

Meanwhile, the Learned Judge has been pondering and he comes up with this triumphant solution:

> *The question, gentlemen—is one of liquor;*
> *You ask for guidance—this is my reply:*
> *He says, when tipsy, he would thrash and kick her,*
> *Let's make him tipsy, gentlemen, and try!*

To this stunningly logical suggestion, there is a mixed response. Counsel objects, Plaintiff objects—but the Defendant says brightly, "I don't object." He is outnumbered, however, when the whole Court choruses, "With all respect/We do object!"

At this the Learned Judge, who has given the knotty problem his best deliberation and likes his proffered solution, tosses his books and papers about in a frenzy of frustration. He obviously has better fish to fry elsewhere and hates to have to spend one more minute at this law business. Angrily he turns on the Court:

> *All the legal furies seize you!*
> *No proposal seems to please you,*
> *I can't stop up here all day,*
> *I must shortly go away.*

Then he orders the barristers and the attorneys to go home and, by way of indicating how little he cares for the Court's officials, he adds:

> *Gentle, simple-minded Usher,*
> *Get you, if you like to Russher . . .*

and in a final burst of self-serving impatience:

> *Put your briefs upon the shelf,*
> *I will marry her myself!*

With this stroke, worthy of Solomon, having cut through all the legalities he is free to come down from the Bench and embrace Angelina.

The opera doesn't end on that obvious, happy note, though. Gilbert leaves us with a few afterthoughts from each of the characters. Angelina declaims that she has found "joy unbounded/With wealth surrounded." Her Counsel, naturally, is happy to see his

The barristers, attorneys, and members of the Court, "With all respect," object to the Judge's suggestion that they make the Defendant tipsy and observe his behavior to Angelina.

"Though homeward as you trudge,/You declare my law is fudge,/Yet of beauty I'm a judge./And a good Judge too!"

The trial ends with a wealthy catch for the pretty Plaintiff and a pessimistic forecast from the faithless Defendant.

lovely client well settled, though perhaps he thinks a little wistfully of her and the Judge on a romantic honeymoon, with: "To castle moated/Away they go." It is Edwin who sounds the true Gilbertian note of a realism that verges on the cynical, though he only leaves it as a question hanging in the air:

> *I wonder whether*
> *They'll live together*
> *In marriage tether*
>   *In manner true?*

No sentimental living-happily-forever-after for W. S. Gilbert!

But the opera ends with the Learned Judge getting high marks for at least one small judgmental talent.

> JUDGE. *Yes, I am a Judge.*
> ALL.   *And a good Judge too!* . . .
>
> JUDGE. *Though homeward as you trudge,*
>   *You declare my law is fudge.*
>   *Yet of beauty I'm a judge.*
> ALL.   *And a good Judge too!*

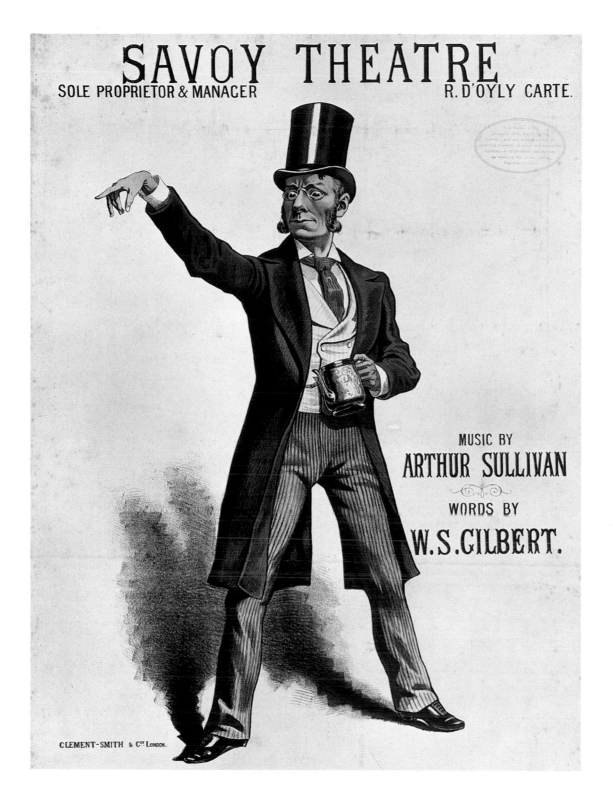

SAVOY THEATRE

SOLE PROPRIETOR & MANAGER   R. D'OYLY CARTE.

MUSIC BY
ARTHUR SULLIVAN

WORDS BY
W. S. GILBERT.

CLEMENT-SMITH & C?? LONDON.

THE SORCERER

After the success of *Trial by Jury,* D'Oyly Carte was eager to put another Gilbert and Sullivan work on the boards as soon as possible. His dream of presenting English comic operas that would surpass the popular French *opéra bouffe* now seemed possible. But in spite of managerial urging and critical encouragement, more than two and a half years were to pass before the curtain rose on the next Gilbert and Sullivan collaboration, *The Sorcerer.* When it finally did, the foundations of a great company were firmly established.

In the interim both men were busy with their separate pursuits. Sullivan, with money coming in from his hit, took off for the Italian lakes with several of the titled friends he was so fond of cultivating, while Gilbert returned to his favorite occupation—writing and producing plays.

Desperate to produce another Gilbert and Sullivan work quickly, Carte was forced by the collaborators' demands for "cash down" to become what he was always meant to be—an impresario. He rounded up four well-to-do backers, became Managing Director of the Comedy Opera Company, leased the Opéra Comique theater on the Strand, and lost no time in approaching Gilbert and Sullivan, money in hand, for a new two-act opéra. Sullivan evidently had a head for business as keen as his ear for music, and he wrote to Carte on behalf of Gilbert and himself that they wanted an advance of £210 on delivery of the manuscript, words and music, and £6.6 a performance royalty for the London run. The "musical comedy" was to be ready for performance by late September, 1877.

Early in 1877 Sullivan's brother Fred died, and in his grief Arthur had written "The Lost Chord," a solemn song that was taken straight to the hearts of sentimental Victorians, who made it the most popular ballad of its time. For some months thereafter Sullivan had difficulty composing. Finally he forced himself to deal with the score for *The Sorcerer.* By his own admission, he "slaved at this work" from April to November, and at last was satisfied that the music was "very pretty and good."

Frank Chappell, the music publisher, was one of the four original directors of the Comedy Opera Company. Chappell's sheet music, with lithographed scenes from the operas, reached a vast and enthusiastic audience.

"Oh! my name is John Wellington Wells, / I'm a dealer in magic and spells . . ."

Gilbert had an easier time with his libretto since, once again, he found his subject in a piece he had written previously. "An Elixir of Love" was a short story illustrated by Gilbert as "Bab" of *The Bab Ballads*, published the year before in *The Graphic*. Magic and love potions were popular in nineteenth-century romantic operas and ballets, from Wagner's *Tristan und Isolde* to Donizetti's *L'Elisir d'Amore*, but Gilbert's version, renamed *The Sorcerer*, was anti-romantic and English to the core.

Breaking new ground in the musical theater involved not just the writing and composing of a different kind of light opera, but an entirely original approach to the casting and staging of each piece. And here the third member of the theatrical triumvirate had a great share in the Gilbert and Sullivan successes. It was D'Oyly Carte's

Vicar Daly, Mrs. Partlet, Alexis and Aline, and Sir Marmaduke Pointdextre— before the Sorcerer's love philter has played havoc with all of them.

genius not only to recognize the potential of their collaboration but, having provided the backing and the theater for their productions, to stand back and give the two geniuses complete artistic freedom.

For *The Sorcerer* there was some slight argument between author and composer over the casting. Not surprisingly, Gilbert wanted the best actors whereas Sullivan wanted the best singers; but with a little give-and-take they assembled a fine company, many of whom were to remain with them for more than a quarter of a century.

Both men were in complete agreement that the role of John Wellington Wells, the "dealer in magic and spells," required an actor with a lightning tongue, perfect diction, with perhaps just a touch of the eccentric. He had to be able to hold a melody line but he didn't need to be a Caruso. Sullivan spotted just the man at an amateur performance of *Trial by Jury* and sent Gilbert after him.

George Grossmith earned his living as a crime reporter at Bow Street Police Court, but for recreation he liked to entertain, singing songs at the piano. When Gilbert approached the slight, bony little man about playing the title role in *The Sorcerer,* Grossmith was astonished. "But Mr. Gilbert," he said, "I should have thought you required a good-looking fellow with a fine voice."

"That," Gilbert replied, "is exactly what we don't want." Ignoring a telegram from the backers of the Comedy Opera Company —"Whatever you do don't engage Grossmith"—Gilbert did precisely that.

The actor was an overnight sensation, eventually becoming the greatest comic star in the Gilbert and Sullivan Company. In every Gilbert and Sullivan opera that followed there was sure to be a part for Grossmith and some of the other *Sorcerer* artists. The pretty young soprano, the handsome tenor, the portly baritone, the mature and homely contralto, the glib-tongued comic actor recur in different guises but it would be part of the unique character of the operas that every role was custom built—like a tailor-made suit—for the artist who was going to play it. As time went on, those famous bygone artists have had their distinguished successors—who bring us Gilbert and Sullivan today, true to the grand tradition.

Lady Sangazure arrives at the Pointdextre estate with her daughter Aline, whose betrothal to Alexis will link two aristocratic old families.

THE SORCERER

ACT I: *Exterior of Sir Marmaduke's Elizabethan mansion. Midday.*

IT IS A FESTIVE DAY FOR VILLAGERS and titled families alike, for Sir Marmaduke Pointdextre's heir, Alexis, is to be formally betrothed to Aline, the only daughter of Lady Sangazure. On the lawns before the Pointdextre country estate, a rosy-brick Elizabethan pile, the villagers in peasant dress lark about in rural merrymaking. "Ring forth, ye bells," they sing—but here the "clarion sound" is pure English, with no sly reference to foreign bells as in the opening scene of *Trial by Jury.*

Gilbert's fun with names is immediately evident. His aristocrats are called Pointdextre: *point,* one of the divisions of a heraldic shield, and *dexter,* the right side of such a shield. And Sangazure: blue blood, indeed! And after the villagers have announced the betrothal and danced off, we meet Mrs. Partlet: the proper name of the hen in Chaucer's "Nun's Priest's Tale," but also a contemptuous name for a woman. (Gilbert was uncharitable, to say the least, in his treatment of middle-aged female characters. Here is one of the earliest examples.)

Mrs. Partlet, like the good mother hen she is, fusses over her daughter Constance, who, in the midst of all the jollity is in a strange depression. Why? Constance answers with a wistful aria about a man whose presence makes her sigh with pleasure, whose absence makes her sigh with grief, but it is a hopeless love. And then as Dr. Daly, the stout Vicar of Ploverleigh, appears in the distance, Constance whispers, "Hush, mother! He is here!" The plot thickens.

Mrs. Partlet, delighted with her daughter's choice, will offer no objection. "Take him—he's yours," she says enthusiastically. "But, mother dear, he is not yours to give!" answers the practical Constance.

Meanwhile, across the lawn Dr. Daly, his old heart stirred by the amatory celebrations, launches into a nostalgic ballad about the time when he and Love were "well acquainted":

Dramatis Personae:

SIR MARMADUKE POINTDEXTRE, an Elderly Baronet (Bass-baritone)

ALEXIS, of the Grenadier Guards—His Son (Tenor)

DR. DALY, Vicar of Ploverleigh (Baritone)

NOTARY (Bass)

JOHN WELLINGTON WELLS, of J. W. Wells & Co., Family Sorcerers (Baritone)

LADY SANGAZURE, a Lady of Ancient Lineage (Contralto)

ALINE, Her Daughter—Betrothed to Alexis (Soprano)

MRS. PARTLET, a Pew-Opener (Contralto)

CONSTANCE, Her Daughter (Soprano)

Chorus of Villagers

First produced at the Opéra Comique on November 17, 1877.

Alexis sighs, "At last we are alone! My darling, you are now irrevocably betrothed to me."

The chorus of villagers outside Sir Marmaduke's mansion sings, "Ring forth, ye bells, / With clarion sound— / Forget your knells, / For joys abound."

Mrs. Partlet and her daughter Constance have matrimonial designs on the unsuspecting Dr. Daly—who believes he is too old to marry now.

Time was, when maidens of the noblest station,
*   Forsaking even military men,*
Would gaze upon me, rapt in adoration—
*   Ah me, I was a fair young curate then!*

Gilbert had taken a firm hand in the casting of this key part and once again overrode the Comedy Opera directors, insisting upon a little-known member of a semi-professional touring company whose forte was melodrama. "He's a staid solid swine, and that's what I want," Gilbert said in describing Rutland Barrington. He was all too aware of the risks involved in what *Punch* was to call the "bold idea of placing a real live burlesque Vicar on the stage." As a matter of fact, when the nervous Barrington approached him shortly before opening night, worrying about the introduction of "a Dean into comic opera" and afraid that the public would hoot him off the stage forever, he later recalled in his autobiography that Gilbert "was very sympathetic, but his reply, 'I quite agree with you,' left me in a state of uncertainty."

Dr. Daly is a pompous and obtuse character, who, upon being accosted by Mrs. Partlet and Constance, completely fails to recognize their designs on him. When Mrs. Partlet confides that she's afraid she'll soon lose Constance, the Vicar asks if she's delicate. Told that young girls look to get married, the light dawns and he says, "Oh, I take you. . . . But when the time *does* come, I shall have much pleasure in marrying her myself—" Constance is in rapture—but only until the Vicar continues, "To some strapping young fellow in her own rank of life."

Constance then is devastated and when she and her mother take their sorrowful leave, the Vicar observes, "Poor little girl! I'm afraid she has something on her mind." But he has no time to puzzle it out, for Alexis, splendid in the red and black and gold uniform of a Grenadier Guard, and Sir Marmaduke, even more splendid in lordly knee breeches and pale brocade, join him.

Sir Marmaduke, who admires "the old school of stately compliment" and would be "obleeged" to have a fair copy of Dr. Daly's flowery congratulations, is proud of his son's Sangazure fiancée. "Aline is rich, and she comes of a sufficiently old family, for she is the seven thousand and thirty-seventh in direct descent from Helen of Troy. True, there was a blot on the escutcheon of that lady—that affair with Paris—but where is the family, other than my own, in which there is no flaw?"

He then lets drop, almost in passing, that fifty years ago he madly loved Lady Sangazure and she loved him. (Was it that blot on her escutcheon that put off a Pointdextre match?) He tells this only to point out that they were more discreet in their declarations than young people today, and he burlesques the effusive "Oh, my adored one!" "Beloved boy!" that later will be Alexis's and Aline's love duet, as he sings their tenor and soprano melody in a bass-baritone.

When Aline and Lady Sangazure join the men, Sir Marmaduke

and the Lady "exhibit signs of strong emotion at the sight of each other, which they endeavor to repress." But the young couple rush into each other's arms with unbridled enthusiasm, using the very exclamations that Sir Marmaduke had just been making fun of.

The two parents perform a stately minuet, carefully keeping their feelings in check—except for asides to the audience delivered "with frantic vehemence," the fire beneath the ice:

Wild with adoration!
Mad with fascination! . . .

Goaded to distraction
By maddening inaction,
I find some satisfaction
  In apostrophe like this:
  "Sangazure immortal,
  Sangazure divine" . . .

Finally the Notary arrives with the marriage contract, which is "prepared for sealing and for signing" and "drafted as agreed," and the lovers are asked: "With hand and seal come execute the deed!" In the Notary's quatrain, Gilbert's legal training has added this note of fussy authenticity.

Now one would think that the opera has run its course; the young lovers are legally affianced, and what else could possibly remain? That would be to reckon without Gilbert's puckish turn of mind.

He was fascinated with stories of magic bullets, love potions, charmed lozenges, and the like and would have used plots employing them more often, but Sullivan and Carte prevailed on him not to. Once was enough. In *The Sorcerer,* not merely the two lovers will be affected by the elixir, as in *Tristan und Isolde.* That would have been picayune for Gilbert, who lavished the magic philter on the entire village, and at the beginning of Act II has the stage asprawl with enchanted men and women.

So, after the Notary, their parents, and the villagers leave Alexis and Aline alone at last, the plot takes a Gilbertian twist. Alexis would like to see the whole world as happy in love as they are, regardless of "the artificial barriers of rank, wealth, education, age, beauty, habits, taste, and temper." He proclaims: "True love should be independent of external influences."

Alexis describes how he has lectured on the subject to mechanics and navvies, in beershops, workhouses, and lunatic asylums, and has addressed these lower-class men on the advantages they would have if they married ladies of rank. "Not a navvy dissented!" he reports proudly.

"Noble fellows!" Aline responds to this. "And what do the countesses say?"

But Alexis is so carried away by his "noble principles" of universal married love that he has hired the firm of J. W. Wells & Co., the

"Time was when Love and I were well acquainted. . . . Ah me, I was a pale young curate then!"

old-established Family Sorcerers in St. Mary Axe, to distribute their love philter throughout the village. "There will not be an adult in the place who will not have learnt the secret of pure and lasting happiness," he tells Aline. "What do you say to that?"

And Aline says, "Well, dear, of course a filter is a very useful thing in a house; but still I don't quite see that it is the sort of thing that places its possessor on the very pinnacle of earthly joy." Gilbert's puns were outrageous but the Victorian audiences adored them.

They also laughed at his visual jokes, like the page named Hercules, who was the tiniest boy Gilbert could find. Hercules brings on the Sorcerer, who in turn brings down the house.

John Wellington Wells introduces himself in a famous patter song sung trippingly on the tongue:

Oh! my name is John Wellington Wells,
I'm a dealer in magic and spells . . .

We keep an extremely small prophet, a prophet
*   Who brings us unbounded returns:*
*   For he can prophesy*
*   With a wink of his eye,*
*   Peep with security*
*   Into futurity,*
*   Sum up your history,*
*   Clear up a mystery,*
*   Humour proclivity*
*   For a nativity—for a nativity;*
*   With mirrors so magical,*
*   Tetrapods tragical,*
*   Bogies spectacular,*
*   Answers oracular,*
*   Facts astronomical,*
*   Solemn or comical,*
*   And if you want it, he*
*   Makes a reduction on*
*   taking a quantity! . . .*

If any one anything lacks,
He'll find it all ready in stacks,
*   If he'll only look in*
*   On the resident Djinn*
Number seventy, Simmery Axe!

Alexis and Aline rush into each other's arms. "Ecstatic rapture!" "Unmingled joy!"

Sir Marmaduke and Lady Sangazure exhibit signs of strong emotion at the sight of each other.

"To love for money all the world is prone:
Some love themselves, and live all lonely:
Give me the love that loves for love alone—
I love that love—I love it only!"

At the engagement tea, Alexis, Aline,
and the Sorcerer watch the guests who
drink Mr. Wells's love philter.

John Wellington Wells, as first played by George Grossmith, was an immediate hit. He was the very model of a Cockney tradesman, energetic, highly respectable in his dubious business, with a sales pitch for his love philters not unlike a wine merchant's: "In buying a quantity, sir, we should strongly advise you taking it in the wood, and drawing it off as you happen to want it. We have it in four-and-a-half and nine gallon casks—also in pipes and hogsheads for laying down, and we deduct 10 per cent for prompt cash."

Alexis, the elegant Grenadier Guard, says, "I should mention that I am a member of the Army and Navy Stores." To which the Sorcerer's businesslike rejoinder is: "In that case we deduct 25 per cent." (The joke here is that the Army and Navy Stores, far from being official or exclusive, were just an inexpensive commercial chain.)

Gilbert had impressed upon his players that it was "absolutely essential to the success of [his comic work] that it should be played with the most perfect earnestness and gravity throughout. . . . Directly the actors show that they are conscious of the absurdity of their utterances the piece begins to drag."

John Wellington Wells in his top hat and frock coat, proud of his "old-established house with a large family connection," must have struck a responsive chord in every solid Victorian businessman in the audience. He manages to be dignified even as he dashes to and fro across the darkening stage with his large teapot full of love philter, singing his weird incantation to all the spirits, demons, hags, imps, and ghosts that Gilbert's imagination could conjure.

At last the stage grows light again, the villagers and all the families and friends reappear, ready to partake of the festive engagement tea as they sing the rollicking

Now to the banquet we press;
    Now for the eggs, the ham;
Now for the mustard and cress,
    Now for the strawberry jam!

Mr. Wells fills everyone's teacup from his magical pot, and in a short time all are rubbing their eyes and staggering about as if under the influence of some kind of drug. Only Alexis, Aline, and Mr. Wells have refrained from drinking the philter, and they watch as one by one all the townspeople fall insensible to the ground.

ACT II: *Exterior of Sir Marmaduke's mansion. Midnight.*
        (Twelve hours are supposed to elapse between Acts I and II.)

IT IS THE MYSTIC HOUR OF TWELVE, and Mr. Wells on tiptoe, followed by Alexis and Aline, comes by moonlight to survey the results of the magic potion. The slumbering forms have yet to feel its full effects.

Sir Marmaduke, Lady Sangazure, Dr. Daly, and the Notary have been removed to the house because, as Mr. Wells explains:

Sir Marmaduke's mansion by moonlight, where the drinkers of the potion lie insensible on the ground.

"Why, where be oi, and what be oi a doin',
A sleepin' out, just when the dews du rise?"

I did not think it meet to see
A dame of lengthy pedigree,
A Baronet and K.C.B.,
A Doctor of Divinity,
And that respectable Q.C.,*
All fast asleep, al-fresco-ly,
And so I had them taken home
And put to bed respectably!

* Queen's Counsel. Wells is promoting the Notary, either through ignorance or goodwill.

In this very class-conscious opera the differences between villagers and their betters are sharply drawn, not only in their dress and language but in distinctions such as this. Alexis, himself well aware of these "artificial barriers," hopes to break them down by means of the chance mismatchings that will result from the Sorcerer's magic. Yet his innate snobbishness surfaces when he congratulates the Cockney Wells, who is in trade, with

Sir, you have acted with discrimination,
And shown more delicate appreciation
Than we expect in persons of your station.

The sleepers begin to stir, and Wells suggests that the young couple and he retire "While Love, the Housemaid, lights her kitchen fire!" As they tiptoe off, the villagers stretch, yawn, rub their eyes, and at last sit up. They speak in the comical West Country accents, and talk of homely things very much like some of Shakespeare's beloved bumpkins:

"But stay— they waken, one by one—
The spell has worked—the deed is done!"

MEN. *Eh, what a nose,*
   And eh, what eyes, miss!
  Lips like a rose,
   And cheeks likewise, miss!

GIRLS. *Oi tell you true,*
   Which I've never done, sir,
  Oi like you
   As I never loiked none, sir! . . .

MEN. *If you'll marry me, I'll dig for you and rake for you!*
GIRLS. *If you'll marry me, I'll scrub for you and bake for you!*

The country boys and girls fall in love the instant they lay eyes on one another, with no complications. But now Constance appears, and her earlier dejection has given way to out-and-out tears. No wonder. She is leading the elderly Notary, who carries an ear-trumpet, and while she remembers her earlier love for the Vicar, she is at the same time helplessly in thrall to her companion.

But when I saw this plain old man,
Away my old affection ran—
  I found I loved him madly.

Unhappy Constance ticks off all the Notary's s
a short list—and then turns to him with a cruel cc

> *You're everything that I detest,*
>   *But still I love you dearly!*

The poor old Notary, straining at his ear-trumpet, sings gamely:

> *I caught that line, but for the rest,*
>   *I did not hear it clearly!*

For much of this time Alexis and Aline have been observing
the scene, overjoyed at the apparent success of the charm.
Aline marvels at how happy they all seem in spite of
matches that the world would consider ill-advised.
Alexis believes they are far wiser than the world
and that now it only remains for the two of them
to drink the philter. In vain Aline tries to reassure
him of her constant and undying love, which
makes the potion unnecessary. Finally she has
to refuse flatly to drink it: "If you cannot
trust me, you have no right to love me—
no right to be loved *by* me."

*Under the spell of the
potion, Aline and Dr.
Daly see each other and
fall helplessly in love.*

John Wellington Wells undoes his magic and disappears in a flash of fire, leaving the happy celebrants to rejoin their old lovers at a rollicking banquet.

George Grossmith as the original John Wellington Wells—from an Illustrated Sporting and Dramatic News *drawing.*

The Reverend Daly arrives as a distraction at this tense moment. He is thoroughly puzzled because this village, which "has not hitherto been addicted to marrying," has just come to him in a body asking him to officiate at a mass wedding. Even Sir Marmaduke seems to be a candidate. Aline and Alexis are pleased to think that a union between her mother and his father will take place at last.

But no, Sir Marmaduke appears with none other than Mrs. Partlet on his arm—something of a shock to everyone. Alexis sportingly tells him that "any wife of yours is a mother of mine," but adds in an aside to Aline that it isn't quite what he could have wished.

Sir Marmaduke describes his bride-to-be as "No high-born exacting beauty . . . But a wife who'll do her duty," while Mrs. Partlet stoutly defends herself as "no saucy minx and giddy . . . But a clean and tidy widdy"—some Gilbertian descriptive rhymes that are, in themselves, almost worth the price of admission.

But now J. W. Wells is beginning to grow alarmed at the misalliances his potion has created. Lady Sangazure, upon first clapping her eyelids on Wells, cries out, "What is this fairy form I see before me?" In vain the Cockney Sorcerer sums up his social disadvantages for the Lady, begging her to hate him as he catalogs his lower-class faults, but she is willing to jettison her upper-class grammar, manners, and prejudices for him in one of the most amusing duets in the opera.

Meanwhile, to please Alexis, Aline finally drinks the philter and hurries to meet him and seal their love even more firmly. But instead she encounters plump Dr. Daly playing on a flageolet. They see one another, and fall hopelessly in love. When Alexis arrives, he is furious at Aline's perfidy, in spite of her piteous "I could not help it!"

Alexis appeals to John Wellington Wells for a solution to these multiple problems and the Sorcerer says that either he or Alexis will have to "yield up his life to Ahrimanes," a Zoroastrian spirit of evil. "I should have no hesitation in sacrificing my own life to spare yours, but"—and here is Gilbert's caricature of the typical tradesman— "we take stock next week, and it would not be fair on the Co."

But the decision is left, democratically, for the majority to make and they sentence the Sorcerer, as the source of all the trouble, to descend to the nether region. "So be it! I submit!" he cries.

All of the mixed-up couples now separate and rejoin their old lovers: Sir Marmaduke and Lady Sangazure, Aline and Alexis, Dr. Daly and Constance, together at last—and the Notary and Mrs. Partlet! As they all prepare for Sir Marmaduke's banquet, singing

Now for the tea of our host—
Now for the rollicking bun—
Now for the muffin and toast—
Now for the gay Sally Lunn!

the Sorcerer disappears in a flash of red fire, a fittingly dramatic end for a most unusual character.

OR THE LASS THAT LOVED A SAILOR

Buoyed by the success of *The Sorcerer*, and with D'Oyly Carte's Comedy Opera Company and the Opéra Comique theater at their disposal, Gilbert and Sullivan lost no time in putting another opera on the stage. *The Sorcerer* played until May 22, 1878, and three days later the curtain went up on the launching of the good ship *Pinafore*, which sailed through a victorious run of twenty-three months in London.

Such speed of composition and production was possible because Gilbert now had a company of players whose style and gifts were particularly suited to the quirky characters he did best. Having had his fun with law courts in *Trial by Jury* and English country society in *The Sorcerer*, he now turned his satirical eye on a third hallowed institution, the British Navy.

Gilbert's father had been a naval surgeon, and family tradition had it that they were descended from Sir Humphrey Gilbert, the navigator who landed in Newfoundland in 1583 and, under Queen Elizabeth's flag, established a first English colony in the New World. In any case, Gilbert loved the sea, and many of his "Bab Ballads" had nautical themes. Since he was addicted to the minor vice of borrowing from his own material, at least four of the ballads inspired characters and situations in this new opera.

By the end of December, 1877, Gilbert had an outline of the opera, which he sent to Sullivan, then in Nice indulging his gambling mania. "I hope & think you will like it," Gilbert wrote to "Dear Sullivan" (throughout their long partnership they never addressed each other by first name). ". . . I should like to have talked it over with you as there is a good deal of fun in it which I haven't set down on paper. Among others a song (kind of 'Judge's Song') for the First Lord—tracing his career as office boy . . . clerk, traveller, junior partner & First Lord of Britain's Navy. . . . Of course there will be no personality in this, the fact that the First Lord in the opera is a *radical* of the most pronounced type will do away with any suspicion that

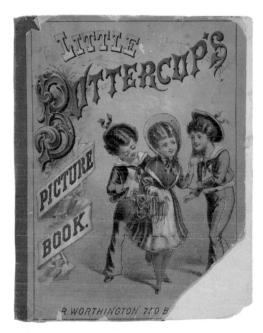

The craze for H.M.S. Pinafore *extended to children, for whom picture books such as this and even a juvenile Miniature Pinafore Opera Company were created.*

W. H. [William Henry] Smith is intended.'' Probably a Gilbertian jest, as the satirization of the landlubber newsboy turned publishing executive, who was appointed First Lord of the Admiralty by Disraeli, was immediately apparent to one and all. And forever after, that man was labeled ''Pinafore Smith.''

Sullivan rose from the gaming tables to the occasion, and in less than five months delivered one of the most charming, sparkling scores of the repertoire. Turning away from the French and Italian styles of most previous comic operas, Sullivan's music draws on English sea chanties, hornpipes, and buoyant tunes that are ir-

Captain Corcoran, disguised in a cloak, carries that infamous naval chastiser, the cat-o'-nine-tails.

resistibly hummed by departing audiences. Yet Sullivan later disclosed: ''It is, perhaps, rather a strange fact that the music to *Pinafore*, which was thought to be so merry and spontaneous, was written while I was suffering agonies from a cruel illness [kidney stones]. I would compose a few bars, and then be almost insensible from pain. . . . Never was music written under such disturbing conditions.''

Having an inspired libretto and score was not enough for the perfectionist collaborators. Six weeks before *Pinafore*'s opening, they went to the great naval base of Portsmouth, where Nelson's flagship, the *Victory*, was at anchor. They were given favored treatment and taken aboard the old warship, where Gilbert's facility as a cartoonist enabled him to make sketches and diagrams that he later translated into a half-inch scale model of the quarterdeck, using colored wooden blocks to represent the characters. He had a miniature theater at his home, and here he worked out the setting and placement of characters and chorus so meticulously that by the time rehearsals were called, Gilbert was thoroughly prepared.

Because in *Pinafore* Gilbert was burlesquing the Navy, it was doubly important that the well-known institution he was turning upside down be presented with the utmost accuracy. D'Oyly Carte went so far as to have the uniforms made by one of Portsmouth's leading naval tailors. By opening night everything was shipshape.

Pinafore was not a smash success at the beginning. In spite of good reviews, business was slack, perhaps because of an extraordinary heat wave. The Comedy Opera Company directors posted closing notices six times; six times Carte countermanded them and kept the ship afloat. Then Sullivan, who was conducting the popular Promenade Concerts at Covent Garden, put a selection of songs from *H. M. S. Pinafore* on one of the programs. London went crazy for the opera. Barrel organs ground out the salty tunes, errand boys whistled them, Society danced to them, and the sheet music sold thousands of copies each day. The newspaper headlines blazoned: ''PINAFORE MANIA!''—and Gilbert at last had enough money to indulge his long-standing passion for the sea. He bought a yacht.

''*You can't expect a chap with such a name as Dick Deadeye to be a popular character—now can you?*''

H.M.S. PINAFORE

or THE LASS THAT LOVED A SAILOR

Act I: *Noon. Quarterdeck of the H.M.S.* Pinafore, *off Portsmouth.*

ON THE QUARTERDECK OF THE *Pinafore* at anchor in Portsmouth Harbor, a rollicking crew of sailors led by Bill Bobstay, their boatswain, go briskly about all their morning chores, polishing the brasswork, splicing rope, climbing the rigging. "So perfect a quarterdeck . . . has assuredly never been put upon the stage. Every block and rope to the minutest detail is in its place . . . an exact model of what it represents. . . . Here we find that marvel of marvels, a chorus that acts, and adds to the reality of the illusion," wrote the critic of *The Standard* in an admiring review.

In their 1840 sailor suits, the sailors must have reminded London audiences of the maritime glory days to which they were heir. And the tars' opening song sets the mood of purposeful frivolity:

> *We sail the ocean blue,*
> *And our saucy ship's a beauty;*
> *We're sober men and true,*
> *And attentive to our duty.*

There is a welcome interruption to their work when Little Buttercup, a buxom bumboat woman, comes aboard with her basket of goodies. This "rosiest," "roundest," and "reddest beauty in all Spithead" sings out her wares in Sullivan's lilting waltz that is another of the opera's hit songs. As one of the "Songs of a Savoyard" added to a later edition of Gilbert's *The Bab Ballads*, "The Bumboat Woman's Story" tells of Buttercup and her romance with a naval officer. After the sailors have crowded round her, buying all her goods, she sounds the first minor note in the merry morning when she asks the Boatswain: ". . . hast ever thought that beneath a gay and frivolous exterior there may lurk a canker-worm which is slowly but surely eating its way into one's very heart?"

The Boatswain has not, but Dick Deadeye has. The ill-favored

Dramatis Personae:

THE RT. HON. SIR JOSEPH PORTER, K.C.B., First Lord of the Admiralty (Baritone)

CAPTAIN CORCORAN, Commanding H.M.S. *Pinafore* (Baritone)

TOM TUCKER, Midshipmite

RALPH RACKSTRAW, Able Seaman (Tenor)

DICK DEADEYE, Able Seaman (Bass)

BILL BOBSTAY, Boatswain (Baritone)

BOB BECKET, Boatswain's Mate—Carpenter (Bass)

JOSEPHINE, the Captain's Daughter (Soprano)

HEBE, Sir Joseph's First Cousin (Mezzo-soprano)

MRS. CRIPPS, Little Buttercup, a Portsmouth Bumboat Woman (Contralto)

Chorus of First Lord's Sisters, His Cousins, His Aunts, Sailors, Marines, etc.

First produced at the Opéra Comique on May 25, 1878.

"The smartest lad in all the fleet—Ralph Rackstraw"—singing his madrigal.

misshapen seaman pushes through the crowd of sailors, who recoil from him in disgust at his ugliness. Philosopher as well as villain, Dick notes that ''From such a face and form as mine the noblest sentiments sound like the black utterances of a depraved imagination. It is human nature—I am resigned.''

But now the smartest lad in all the fleet—Ralph (pronounced *Rafe*) Rackstraw—comes on deck, singing a melancholy madrigal whose last line describes his problem neatly: ''I love—and love, alas, above my station!'' Since he also loves a lass above his station, this is rather a well-fitting pun—for those who like them.

The problem of class distinctions and station, dealt with in the stratified country society of *The Sorcerer*, appears again in *Pinafore*, where the caste system of naval rank, high and low birth, and self-made arrivistes are given their comeuppance. Once again love may be the great leveler, and we will see whether the Captain's daughter will have anything to do with a lowly born suitor. But even Dick Deadeye, the realist, knows that ''captains' daughters don't marry fore-mast hands.''

When the gallant Captain Corcoran appears, he is not unlike *The Bab Ballads'* worthy Captain Reece, who ''was adored by all his men.'' A good-looking product of the Royal Navy, the Captain is resplendent in full ceremonial uniform from cocked hat to epaulettes and sword. His rapport with his crew is obvious, as is his pride: ''I am the Captain of the *Pinafore*. . .'' he sings, and he lists all of his nautical accomplishments, among them that he is ''never, never sick at sea!''

ALL.　*What, never?*
CAPT.　*No, never!*
ALL.　*What,* never?
CAPT.　*Hardly ever!*
ALL.　*He's hardly ever sick at sea!*
　　　Then give three cheers, and one cheer more,
　　　For the hardy Captain of the Pinafore!

He also ''hardly ever swears a big, big D''—thus eliciting another round of cheers from his admiring crew ''For the well-bred Captain of the *Pinafore!*''

But Captain Corcoran, too, nurtures a secret sorrow. His daughter Josephine is sought in marriage by no less a personage than Sir Joseph Porter, First Lord of the Admiralty, but the foolish girl doesn't seem to ''tackle kindly'' to the match. Worse yet, when the Captain and his attractive daughter are alone, she confesses that the reason she cannot love Sir Joseph is that her heart is already given (''Sorry her lot who loves too well . . .''). And, most terrible of all is the news that the man she loves is—a common sailor. ''A common sailor? Oh fie!'' her father exclaims.

Then the kindly Captain tries to reason with the girl. He tells her he attaches very little value to wealth or rank—''but the line

''For I'm called Little Buttercup—dear Little Buttercup,
Though I could never tell why,
But still I'm called Buttercup . . .
Sweet Little Buttercup I!''

must be drawn somewhere. A man in that station may be brave and worthy, but at every step he would commit solecisms that society would never pardon." Victorian society's preoccupation with the outward signs of class is here neatly skewered.

While Josephine retires to her cabin to contemplate a photograph of Sir Joseph in the hope of changing her affections, the Captain ascends the poop deck. The crew, who have changed into dress whites, pea jackets, and straw hats to greet the First Lord, tiptoe onto the deck, crowding the rail for a glimpse of the great man's barge carrying his beautiful entourage of sisters, cousins, and aunts out to the ship. The Midshipmite, Tom Tucker, the tiniest boy available, is lifted up the better to see, and he adjusts his little telescope, takes a good squint, and waves excitedly.

The chorus of female voices wafts up to the deck in a delightful barcarolle:

> Over the bright blue sea
> Comes Sir Joseph Porter, K.C.B.,
> Wherever he may go
> Bang-bang the loud nine-pounders go!
> Shout o'er the bright blue sea
> For Sir Joseph Porter, K.C.B.

"Sir Joseph's barge approaches, manned by twelve trusty oarsmen and accompanied by the admiring crowd of sisters, cousins, and aunts that attend him wherever he goes."

The initials stand for Knight Companion of the Most Noble Order of the Bath, after the Garter the highest British honor. And Sir Joseph's first words when he steps on deck indicate his full appreciation of his worth:

> I am the monarch of the sea,
> The ruler of the Queen's Navee . . .

Porter was first played by George Grossmith, made up to resemble Lord Horatio Nelson. His elderly Cousin Hebe (the name, ironically, means "youthful prime") was Jessie Bond, and the original Captain Corcoran was Rutland Barrington. These three formed the nucleus of the first D'Oyly Carte company.

Sir Joseph's patter song summarizes his remarkable rise from attorney's office boy ("And I polished up the handle of the big front door") to pocket borough Member of Parliament ("And I never thought of thinking for myself at all"); and for thinking so little, "they rewarded me/By making me the ruler of the Queen's Navee!" His ultimate advice:

Little Buttercup agrees with Dick Deadeye that he has "a beast of a name" and is "certainly plain."

> Stick close to your desks and never go to sea,
> And you all may be Rulers of the Queen's Navee!

has been bringing down the house for over a century.

Sir Joseph's utter lack of seagoing experience doesn't stop him from taking a didactic stance with the professional naval people, from Captain Corcoran down to "that splendid seaman," Ralph Rackstraw. He teaches the Captain manners and the hornpipe, gives

"Josephine," declares Ralph, "in one brief breath I will concentrate the hopes, the doubts, the anxious fears of six weary months. . . . I am a British sailor, and I love you!"

"I am the monarch of the sea, The ruler of the Queen's Navee . . . But when the breezes blow, I generally go below."

Ralph a song he has composed for the Royal Navy, that will fill them all with his radical ideas of equality ("a British sailor is any man's equal, excepting mine"), and blithely undermines the men's respect for their commanding officer. After which he is off to the Captain's cabin to confer on the tender and sentimental subject that brought him and his entourage to the *Pinafore*.

Ralph, the Boatswain, the Boatswain's Mate, and the rest of *Pinafore*'s crew take up the song that Sir Joseph has given them:

> *A British tar is a soaring soul,*
> *As free as a mountain bird,*
> *His energetic fist should be ready to resist*
> *A dictatorial word . . . .*
>
> *His bosom should heave and his heart should glow,*
> *And his fist be ever ready for a knock-down blow.*

Meanwhile Josephine comes on deck, where Ralph Rackstraw is leaning pensively against the bulwark. Sir Joseph's talk of equality has given him the courage to speak to the Captain's daughter about his love. But when he speaks at last it is in high-flown polysyllables delivered with the fervor of an old-time Shakespearean actor. He winds up his declaration with "I am but a living ganglion of irreconcilable antagonisms. I hope I make myself clear, lady?" The lady, in a histrionic aside, says, "His simple eloquence goes to my heart."

But Josephine is bound by caste to reject the lover she secretly yearns for, so though her asides are an indication of her true feelings, her words to Ralph express haughty disdain:

> *Refrain, audacious tar,*
> *Your suit from pressing,*
> *Remember what you are,*
> *And whom addressing!*

But, to the audience:

> *I'd laugh my rank to scorn*
> *In union holy,*
> *Were he more highly born*
> *Or I more lowly!*

When Josephine returns to her cabin, the despairing suitor calls his messmates together and tells them that Josephine has scorned him and he will take his life. Just as Ralph is putting a loaded pistol to his head, however, Josephine comes running back on deck. "Ah! stay your hand!" she exclaims, rushing to his side. "I love you!"

With the connivance of the sympathetic crew and all of Sir Joseph's sisters, cousins, and aunts, the two lovers plan to steal away that night, get married on shore, and return as man and wife whom no one can part. Everyone is delighted with the plan, but ominous Dick Deadeye tries to remind them of their differences:

One member of Sir Joseph Porter's admiring entourage of sisters, cousins, and aunts.

Remember, she's your gallant captain's daughter,
And you the meanest slave that crawls the water!

But the others will have none of that and chase the spoilsport below deck. Then all give three cheers "for the sailor's bride/Who casts all thought of rank aside," and burst into a reprise of Sir Joseph's song "A British Tar Is a Soaring Soul." The first-act curtain falls on a scene of merriment as all except the now-absent Dick Deadeye, the Captain, and Sir Joseph sing and dance in celebration of the elopement-to-be.

"Let's give three cheers for the sailor's bride
Who casts all thought of rank aside—
Who gives up home and fortune too
For the honest love of a sailor true!"

The quarterdeck of the Pinafore becomes a dance floor for the sailors and Sir Joseph's female relatives in the Act I finale.

ACT II: *Night. Quarterdeck of the H.M.S.* Pinafore, *off Portsmouth.*

IN CONTRAST TO ITS DAYTIME BUSTLE OF ACTIVITY, the *Pinafore's* deck is almost deserted now in the light of a full moon. On the poop deck Captain Corcoran sits alone strumming a mandolin. He is splendid in full naval mess dress—naval-cut tailcoat, black tie, white waistcoat, gold-striped trousers, gold epaulettes, full insignia, and decorations. Unseen by the Captain, Little Buttercup is seated below on the quarterdeck, gazing sentimentally up at him.

The Captain's song is a complaint to the moon, ''Bright regent of the heavens,'' about all the things that have gone wrong suddenly. ''Why,'' he asks, ''is everything/Either at sixes or at sevens?''

When he discovers Little Buttercup, she hints mysteriously that there is a change in store for him:

> *Things are seldom what they seem,*
> *Skim milk masquerades as cream . . .*
>
> *Turbot is ambitious brill;*
> *Gild the farthing if you will,*
> *Yet it is a farthing still.*

Though the puzzled Captain, who seems more than fond of her, says he can never be more than her friend, Buttercup suggests that that too may change. She leaves the Captain thoroughly mystified by everything except her sincere regard for him.

While he is pondering the meaning of her oracular utterances, Sir Joseph joins him. The First Lord, accustomed in his life to rapid success, has had no luck wooing the Captain's daughter and he is ready to throw in his hand. ''I don't think she will do,'' he tells her anxious father. But the Captain assures him that Josephine is probably dazzled by his rank and suggests that if Sir Joseph explains officially that ''it is a standing rule at the Admiralty that love levels all ranks,'' she might accept his offer.

When Sir Joseph passes this information on to Josephine, she lights up. ''I thank you, Sir Joseph. I *did* hesitate, but I will hesitate no longer. (*Aside.*) He little thinks how eloquently he has pleaded his rival's cause!''

And now the First Lord, the Captain, and Josephine launch into a triumphant trio that has, at times, had seven encores:

> *Ring the merry bells on board-ship,*
> *Rend the air with warbling wild,*
> *For the union of* $\begin{Bmatrix} his \\ my \end{Bmatrix}$ *lordship*
> *With a humble captain's child!*
> *For a humble captain's daughter—*
> *For a gallant captain's daughter—*
> *And a lord who rules the water—*

''*Let the air with joy be laden,*
Rend with songs the air above,
For the union of a maiden
With the man who owns her love!''

A handbell, carillon, piano, triangle, carnival sledgehammer-and-gong strength test, telephone, and doorbell have been introduced as part of the zany business as verse follows verse about the merry bells. But only the audience is aware that Josephine, in asides, substitutes, "And a *tar* who ploughs the water!" each time the last line is sung.

Captain Corcoran compliments the First Lord on his eloquence, which has won Josephine. "Your argument was unanswerable." To which the First Lord delivers the stunning exit line "Captain Corcoran, it is one of the happiest characteristics of this glorious country that official utterances are invariably regarded as unanswerable."

The Captain hasn't long to enjoy the Elysian prospect of a daughter the bride of a Cabinet Minister. Dick Deadeye now scutters up to the happy man and tells him that "the merry maiden and the tar," Ralph Rackstraw, are going to run off. The Captain thanks Dick for his warning, and ominously changes the last line of their duet to "The merry cat-o'-nine-tails and the tar." He disguises himself in a mysterious black cloak, hiding his face, while Dick Deadeye cackles, "Ha, ha! They are foiled—foiled—foiled!"

Very soon the crew and Ralph, joined by Little Buttercup and Josephine, tiptoe across the deck, ready for the elopement. Suddenly the Captain, in concealment, stamps his foot, and whacks the cat-o'-nine-tails down on Dick's back. "Why, what was that?" they all ask in alarm. "It was the cat!" Dick reassures them. Once again it happens, and this time the Captain leaps out, throwing off the cloak. "They're right, it was the cat!" he says, stopping them all in their tracks and brandishing the whip.

Ralph, undeterred, declares his love for the Captain's matchless girl. Although he is "humble, poor, and lowly born," he dares aspire to Josephine because—"I am an Englishman!"

As the Boatswain points out: ". . . it's greatly to his credit, / That he is an Englishman!"

> *For he might have been a Roosian,*
> *A French, or Turk, or Proosian,*
> *Or perhaps Itali-an! . . .*
>
> *But in spite of all temptations*
> *To belong to other nations,*
> *He remains an Englishman!*

The Captain is not mollified by this magnificently patriotic sentiment, and he gives vent to his anger with, "Why damme, it's too bad!" At this moment Sir Joseph appears on the poop deck and is horrified to hear the Captain use the "big D." He sends him to his cabin, and when he discovers that Ralph and Josephine love each other ("She is the figurehead of my ship of life," the young man intones), he sends Ralph to the dungeon in chains.

And now the time has come for Little Buttercup to untangle the

"Kind Captain, I've important information,
Sing hey, the kind commander that you are,
About a certain intimate relation,
Sing hey, the merry maiden and the tar."

*"Then give three cheers, and one cheer more
For the former Captain of the* Pinafore.*"*

plot and disclose her secret. She tells how in her charming youth she practiced "baby-farming." She mixed up two tender babes, one of low condition, one upper crust and "A regular patrician." "The well-born babe was Ralph—/ Your captain was the other!!!"

There is general consternation and the two men are brought back on deck. (Somehow the difference in their ages is glossed over for the sake of the plot.) Josephine is stricken to discover that her father is—"a common sailor!" Sir Joseph announces that a marriage with Corcoran's daughter is now out of the question. Love may level ranks "to a considerable extent, but it does not level them as much as that," he says.

So Ralph gets Josephine. "Oh bliss, oh rapture!"

The erstwhile Captain can now suitably marry Little Buttercup. "Oh rapture, oh bliss!"

Sir Joseph, who laments, "Sad my lot and sorry/What shall I do? I cannot live alone!" is taken firmly in hand by First Cousin Hebe; she promptly disposes of the sisters, cousins, and aunts; and the three loving pairs will be united on the same day.

Pinafore ends rousingly with the entire cast singing a reprise of "He Is an Englishman." Is it any wonder audiences took it to their hearts?

THE PIRATES OF PENZANCE

OR THE SLAVE OF DUTY

irates may well have been on W. S. Gilbert's mind after the success of *Pinafore* because of the numerous pirated productions of the hit in the United States, playing without paying one cent of royalty to author, composer, or manager. The three men regretted not only the loss of money, but Sullivan was especially irked that his music was not performed as written, and D'Oyly Carte, after a troubleshooting trip to America, reported: ". . . acting, costumes, time of music, etc. are too atrociously bad for words to express."

Still, the authentic production was coining money in London, and had two authorized touring companies playing all the sizable English towns. After only a year, Gilbert was able to trade in his first yacht for a bigger one, *Pleione*. And it was on her that, with "Mrs.," he sailed the Cornish coast near Penzance and hatched the idea for an opera that would be called *The Pirates of Penzance*.

The three partners had meanwhile won a case against the original backers of their company, who had had the gall to break up a performance of *Pinafore* with a mob of roughs in an attempt to take away the scenery and set up their own rival production in London. The case was won but the company was bankrupt. It was then that Carte–Sullivan–Gilbert set up their remarkable and long-enduring partnership agreement. Written in Gilbert's hand, the document specified that each of the three men put up £1,000 and divide all profits equally, after expenses. Carte drew a salary of £15 per week, while Gilbert and Sullivan each received a fee of four guineas "per representation."

It was an incentive to get on with more operas, and Richard D'Oyly Carte's plan was to open the so-called "New Opera," swathed in secrecy to thwart pirates, in New York—thereby establishing United States copyright. First, though, the team put on the only authorized American production of *H.M.S. Pinafore,* on December 1, 1879, at New York City's Fifth Avenue Theatre to show

In the twentieth century, record albums joined sheet music to bring Gilbert and Sullivan into more homes—and more royalties into the coffers.

"And, to make us more than merry,/Let the pirate bumper pass."

American audiences how the authentic musical was supposed to be played—and also to get a bit of their own back. Later they sent out three road companies of *Pinafore* as well, and while American audiences were becoming attuned to the genuine article, *The Pirates of Penzance* was being readied for its New Year's Eve opening at the same theater, its score locked away in a safe between rehearsals.

Sullivan, always a last-minute composer, had only completed the music for part of Act II when he arrived in New York. He then discovered to his consternation that he had left the Act I libretto and musical settings in London. After getting *Pinafore* on the boards, Sullivan holed up in his New York hotel to reconstruct Act I and finish Act II, sometimes composing through the night after rehearsing all day. By December 31, when the new opera premiered, he was "utterly worn out," and "more dead than alive," but his diary records that when he got to

*"I am the very model of a
modern Major-General,
I've information vegetable,
animal, and mineral,
I know the kings of England,
and I quote the fights
historical . . ."*

the theater, crammed with New York's elite, and took the stick in his hand, he "got better." *The Pirates of Penzance* was, in the weary composer's words, a "grand success."

This was the only Gilbert and Sullivan opera to have its world premiere outside England, and the opening night program at the Fifth Avenue Theatre carried above the title the words "First production of the New Melo-Dramatic Opera, in Two Acts . . . written and composed expressly for production in the United States." In order to protect the British copyright, members of an English D'Oyly Carte touring company in the provinces hastily tied pirate handkerchiefs on their heads and, still in their *Pinafore* sailor costumes, ran through a matinee performance of *Pirates* at the Royal Bijou Theatre in Paignton, near Plymouth, only a few hours before the world premiere in New York. The actors carried their parts, in place of swords.

America lionized Gilbert and Sullivan. They were interviewed, wined, dined, admired, and quoted. Gilbert's reputation as a wit was not diminished by stories such as the one concerning an effusive woman at a reception, who gushed, "Dear Mr Gilbert, your friend Sullivan's music is *too* delightful. It reminds me so much of dear *Baytch*. Do tell me what is *Baytch* doing just now. Is he still composing?" To which Gilbert snapped, "No, madam. Just now dear Bach is by way of decomposing."

Pirates was a rousing success in the United States, earning $4,000 a week for author and composer just for the first six weeks of the New York run, and there were authorized productions in many other cities, crisscrossing the country from Minnesota to Louisiana and from Massachusetts to Nebraska. Carte was diligent in fighting pirated productions and brilliant about licensing authentic ones in distant countries like Australia, as well as in towns and hamlets, to amateur groups, and to every possible source of interest and income. Always the high standards of the company were upheld, so quality was maintained and Gilbert and Sullivan's reputations were as golden as their revenues.

The most operatic of all the Gilbert and Sullivan works, *The Pirates of Penzance* has had a rebirth in its second century in a production sponsored by Joseph Papp and the New York Shakespeare Festival and a consequent film made in England with rock stars, electronic music, and the enthusiasm of rediscovery in a new age.

"Spy"'s Vanity Fair *caricature of a high-ranking military man of the 1880s bears a remarkable resemblance to Gilbert and Sullivan's Major-General.*

THE PIRATES OF PENZANCE

OR THE SLAVE OF DUTY

ACT I: *A rocky seashore on the coast of Cornwall.*

OFF THE ROCKY COAST OF CORNWALL a schooner lies at anchor on the calm sea. In a little cove, a dozen or so pirates are taking their ease, playing cards and drinking, while Samuel, the pirate lieutenant, goes from group to group filling cups from a flask. One young man sits apart, despondent. He is Frederic the apprentice.

The pirates begin to sing, and from the very first line of their chorus we know we are in Gilbert's topsy-turvy world once again. Here is a band of maritime outlaws, rough-and-ready fellows, and what are they saying?

> *Pour, oh, pour the pirate sherry;*
> *Fill, oh, fill the pirate glass . . .*

They are completely in earnest about this most un-piratical drink, fulfilling Gilbert's foreglimpse of the new opera's aim, "similar to . . . *Pinafore,* namely to treat a thoroughly farcical subject in a thoroughly serious manner." It is similar, too, in its dealing with a group of seafaring men and their leader—the story this time set on land and the seafarers outside the law.

The pirates are set up like any self-respecting, legitimate profession in which apprentices are bound to a master for a number of years while learning their trade. Today they are celebrating their apprentice Frederic's twenty-first birthday and, now that he's out of his indentures, his full-fledged membership in the band. The Pirate King himself welcomes the young man to piracy.

But Frederic drops a bombshell into the festivities. He doesn't intend to be a pirate. He has done his best for them as an apprentice because he is "the slave of duty," as the opera's subtitle indicates, but, he explains, it was through an error that he was bound to them as a child.

And now a woman steps forward and we learn to our amazement—and amusement—that the apprentice pirate has had his

Dramatis Personae:

MAJOR-GENERAL STANLEY (Baritone)

THE PIRATE KING (Bass-baritone)

SAMUEL, His Lieutenant (Baritone)

FREDERIC, the Pirate Apprentice (Tenor)

SERGEANT OF POLICE (Bass)

MABEL (Soprano)

EDITH (Mezzo-soprano)

KATE (Mezzo-soprano)   General Stanley's Daughters

ISABEL (Mezzo-soprano)

RUTH, a Pirate Maid of All Work (Contralto)

Chorus of Pirates, Police, and General Stanley's Daughters

First produced at the Fifth Avenue Theatre, New York, on December 31, 1879.

First produced at the Opéra Comique, London, on April 3, 1880.

"Yet, when the danger's near . . . We manage to appear . . . As insensible to fear/As anybody here."

Souvenir cards from a children's production of Pirates *at the Savoy, Christmas 1884.*

nurse with him all those years: Ruth, the Pirate Maid of All Work! She informs the band that when he was a little lad his father asked her to apprentice him to a *pilot*, but she misheard the directions and:

> *I took and bound this promising boy apprentice to a* pirate.
> *A sad mistake it was to make and doom him to a vile lot,*
> *I bound him to a pirate—you—instead of to a pilot.*

Frederic says firmly that this afternoon when his obligation to them ceases he will be duty bound to devote himself "heart and soul" to the pirates' extermination. Because, though individually he loves them, collectively he looks on them with disgust and detestation.

The Pirate King, scanning the sun above the sea's horizon, says that it's only half-past eleven, and until twelve Frederic must still have the pirates' interests at heart. So, would he please tell them why they haven't been able to make piracy pay? Dutifully Frederic points out that they are too tenderhearted. They never molest an orphan because they're orphans themselves, and now that that's got about, well, "The last three ships we took proved to be manned entirely by orphans, and so we had to let them go."

The Pirate King prevails on Frederic to take Ruth with him when he leaves—actually, neither man wants to be burdened with the middle-aged spinster—and Frederic complains that since he was eight years old, hers has been the only female face he's seen, so that he has no basis for comparison. "What . . . if I were to marry this innocent person, and then find out that she is, on the whole, plain!"

When Frederic invites the Pirate King to accompany him back to civilization, that mustachioed swashbuckler turns him down. "I don't think much of our profession, but, contrasted with respectability, it is comparatively honest." And the king launches into his bold apology for his life:

> *Oh better far to live and die*
> *Under the brave black flag I fly,*
> *Than play a sanctimonious part,*
> *With a pirate head and a pirate heart.*
> *Away to the cheating world go you,*
> *Where pirates all are well-to-do;*
> *But I'll be true to the song I sing,*
> *And live and die a Pirate King.*
>   *For I am a Pirate King.*

The pirates go off about their business, leaving Frederic with Ruth, who begs him to take her with him. "You will find me a wife of a thousand!" she promises him. "No, but I shall find you a wife of forty-seven," he answers brutally, "and that is quite enough."

This uncomfortable conversation is interrupted by the sound of clear, girlish voices. Then, over the wild rocks of the Cornish coast, one by one the maids appear. They wear dresses as brightly colored as flowers, poke bonnets frame their faces, and ruffled parasols add a gay, coquettish touch. Sullivan described the scene glowingly: "The *mise-en-scène* and the dresses are something to be dreamed about. I never saw such a beautiful combination of colour and form on any stage . . . some of the girls look as if they had stepped out of a Gainsborough picture." Their song, "Climbing over Rocky Mountain," was taken from Gilbert and Sullivan's first collaboration, *Thespis,* and thrown into the breach here when Sullivan's Act I music was left behind in London. It is all that remains of the *Thespis* music in the opera repertoire.

Frederic is smitten. Then he turns on Ruth, who has deceived him by telling him she is beautiful, and renounces her.

Not wanting these beauties to see him in his alarming pirate costume, the young man hides in a cave while the Major-General's daughters—for that is who they are—sing a little song and, since they believe themselves to be the first human beings to set foot on this enchanting beach, start to remove shoes and stockings so they can paddle barefoot.

Before they can strip their feet bare, honorable Frederic leaps out of the cave because it is his duty to let them know they are not unobserved. The modest young women hop about on one unshod foot while Frederic asks, in a tenderly beautiful song, if there is not one of them—even if homely and with a bad complexion—who would marry him. Only Mabel, appearing suddenly, responds in the affirmative. (Her catty sisters ask in an aside if, "had he not been / A thing of beauty, / Would she be swayed by quite as keen / A sense of duty?") But Mabel's compassion shines through her song to Frederic, "Poor Wandering One," and off they go for a quiet tête-à-tête.

The girls are suddenly surrounded by the stealthy pirates, who, having tiptoed up behind them, seize—each one—a prize. A delightful ensemble song ensues with the pirates singing:

> *Here's a first-rate opportunity*
> *To get married with impunity . . .*

while the girls sing:

> *We have missed our opportunity*
> *Of escaping with impunity . . .*

Before the girls can be "Conjugally matrimonified, / By a doctor of divinity, / Who resides in this vicinity," brave Mabel dresses down the pirates and warns them that she and all the other girls are Wards in Chancery, whose father is a Major-General. The pirates are cowed—and a good thing, too, for there, suddenly in their midst (sometimes he arrives astride a donkey), is Major-General Stanley.

Brushing his military mustache to each side, he inhales deeply before launching into a hell-for-leather patter song at top speed. "I Am the Very Model of a Modern Major-General" is a tongue twister,

"I don't think much of our profession, but, contrasted with respectability, it is comparatively honest. No . . . I shall live and die a Pirate King."

"Climbing over rocky mountain, Skipping rivulet and fountain . . . Climb the hardy little lasses, Till the bright sea-shore they gain!"

"We have missed our opportunity
Of escaping with impunity;
So farewell to the felicity
Of our maiden domesticity!"

"Oh, dry the glistening tear
That dews that martial cheek;
Thy loving children hear,
In them thy comfort seek."

an information compendium, a dazzling technical tour de force, and a sure showstopper. It was probably tailored to George Grossmith's talents, but Martyn Green's later inventive ''business'' was often good for three rousing encores when he sang it.

When the Major-General throws himself on the pirates' mercy by pleading that he is an orphan boy and would be alone in the world if they took his daughters in marriage, the pirates sob, ''Poor fellow!'' dabbing their eyes with big red bandannas. Their king declares they're not devoid of feeling—''For what, we ask, is life/Without a touch of Poetry in it?'' At this, all kneel and sing an *a cappella* hymn to Poetry that reminds the audience that the composer of this comic opera has another fame, for his sacred music (among his hymns are ''Onward, Christian Soldiers'' and ''Rock of Ages'').

The pirates, all orphans themselves, cheer their fellow orphan and elect him and his daughters honorary members of their band. The Major-General is a little uncomfortable that he has had to indulge in an ''innocent fiction,'' but comforts himself with the thought that it is not in the same category as a ''regular terrible story.''

And now everyone is dancing with joy because Frederic and Mabel are to be married and all her sisters will get to be bridesmaids. But there is one unhappy note: Ruth enters and throws herself at Frederic's feet, imploring him to remember her. Frederic cannot forgive her deceiving him, however—and besides, he has a younger and prettier bride-to-be.

While the girls and their father clamber up the rocks to watch, the pirates launch into a wild dance of delight. The Pirate King brandishes a black flag with a skull and crossbones while the Major-General decorously produces a neat Union Jack. Ruth returns to make a final appeal to Frederic, who, for the last time, casts her from him.

ACT II: *A ruined chapel by moonlight.*

IN THE RUINED CHAPEL ON HIS ESTATE, Major-General Stanley sits pensively, surrounded by his daughters. Moonlight streams in from the ruined Gothic windows at the back.

The daughters whom he has saved by a lie from piratical marriages now try to console their conscience-stricken father. Wracked by remorse, he has come to humble himself before the tombs of his ancestors and implore their forgiveness for dishonoring the family escutcheon with a fib.

Frederic sensibly reminds him that since he only bought the property a year ago, he owes nothing to the occupants of these tombs. But by the general's logic, when he bought the chapel and its contents—''in this chapel are ancestors: you cannot deny that''—he became their descendant by purchase. He would make a clean breast of his untruth to the pirates but fears the disastrous consequences. Therefore he is slightly cheered to know that Frederic plans to atone for his involuntary association with the outlaws by mounting an expedition of the local constabulary against the pirates that very night and "sweeping them from the face of the earth." After which Frederic will be able to marry his beloved Mabel with a clear conscience.

The Major-General offers to give the lionhearted escort his blessing, and onto the scene the policemen march in single file, carrying bull's-eye lanterns—the most timid and hesitant group of would-be law enforcers the world has ever seen. They start out bravely

"I come here to humble myself before the tombs of my ancestors, and to implore their pardon for having brought dishonour on the Family escutcheon."

enough; but as their courage flags, they try to work it to the sticking point by singing a sort of trumpet-call talisman, which they pretend to play on their billy clubs:

When the foeman bares his steel,
Tarantara! tarantara!
We uncomfortable feel,
Tarantara!

For when threatened with emeutes,*
Tarantara! tarantara!
And your heart is in your boots,
Tarantara!
There is nothing brings it round,
Tarantara! tarantara!
Like the trumpet's martial sound,
Tarantara! tarantara!

* French for brawls.

"He is a little boy of five! Ha! Ha!
A paradox, a paradox,
A most ingenious paradox!"

While the daughters exhort the police to go to their glory—and should they die in combat, every Cornish daughter will water their graves with her tears—the police, who protest that "Such expressions don't appear,/Calculated men to cheer," sing their own very different melody in reprise. The interplay of the two singing groups, aside from being amusing and advancing the plot, is evidence of Sullivan's remarkably skillful counterpoint.

Finally the police do go, however hesitantly, in quest of the pirates. Before Frederic can follow, however, he is surprised by the arrival of Ruth and the Pirate King, armed with pistols, which they hold to each of his ears. Under the circumstances they are able to persuade Frederic to listen to their startling paradox:

> *We knew your taste for curious quips,*
> *For cranks and contradictions queer,*
> *And with the laughter on our lips,*
> *We wished you there to hear.*
> *We said, "If we could tell it him,*
> *How Frederic would the joke enjoy!"*
> *And so we've risked both life and limb*
> *To tell it to our boy.*

It seems that Frederic had been born on February 29, 1856, in a leap year, and therefore when counting in the usual way he is twenty-one; but reckoning by his actual birthday, he is only five-and-a-quarter. He will not, by that proper reckoning, reach his twenty-first birthday and be out of his indentures until 1940. (How impossibly far in the future that date must have seemed to Victorian audiences!) "A paradox!" "A most ingenious paradox!" The Pirate King and Ruth are in stitches.

Frederic is appalled and protests wildly that they surely will not hold him to the letter of their agreement. Ruth and the Pirate King reply, smugly, that they will leave it to his "sense of duty."

Frederic's enslaving sense of duty compels him not only to continue as a member of the pirate band but to disclose to them that the Major-General lied: he is not an orphan. The Pirate King is furious and vows to attack the castle with his band and kill the traitor that very night. He and Ruth hasten away to round up the other pirates.

When Mabel finds Frederic in tears, he tells her what has happened. She implores him to stay with her rather than continue his indentures. "But when stern Duty calls," he explains, "I must obey." He promises that in 1940 he will return and claim her. "It seems so long!" Mabel says forlornly, as Frederic vaults nimbly out of the chapel window and dashes off to rejoin the pirates.

And now the policemen return, marching in single file, keeping their spirits up with their "Tarantara!" Mabel explains

"In 1940 I of age shall be,
I'll then return, and claim you—I declare it! . . .
Swear that, till then, you will be true to me."

"Tormented with the anguish dread
Of falsehood unatoned,
I lay upon my sleepless bed,
And tossed and turned and groaned."

that young Frederic, who was to have led them to "death and glory" ("That is not a pleasant way of putting it," they protest), has had to rejoin the pirates. She cuts off all criticism of him by maintaining that he has sacrificed to his sense of duty, and she exhorts them to do likewise.

The reluctant police, with their Sergeant, now deliver themselves of their famous lament about being the "agents whereby our erring fellow-creatures are deprived of that liberty which is so dear to all":

> *Our feelings we with difficulty smother—*
> > *'Culty smother*
> *When constabulary duty's to be done—*
> > *To be done.*
> *Ah, take one consideration with another—*
> > *With another,*
> *A policeman's lot is not a happy one.*

Rutland Barrington, the original Sergeant of Police, always had to deliver two encores of this popular song, and he once suggested to Gilbert that he write a special encore verse. Gilbert's testy reply was: "Mr. Barrington, 'encore' means 'sing it again.'"

The pirates are meantime sneaking up on the sleeping household, and the policemen have concealed themselves. The inverted humor of Gilbert and Sullivan has the pirates loudly stamping their feet and singing double-forte:

> *With cat-like tread, (stamp!)*
> > *Upon our prey we steal, (stamp!)*
> *In silence dread (STAMP!)*
> > *Our cautious way we feel. (STAMP!)*

Meanwhile the hidden constabulary whisper, pianissimo, "Tarantara, tarantara!" to keep their spirits up.

The Major-General, too tormented by his bad conscience to sleep, comes to the chapel in nightcap, dressing gown, and socks and slippers, carrying a lighted candle. His daughters, in white peignoirs and nightcaps, and also carrying candles, are worried about him and follow soon after. So all are conveniently gathered when the pirates pounce. Mabel cries, "Frederic, save us!" and her suitor answers nobly, "Beautiful Mabel,/I would if I could, but I am not able." He is being restrained by two pirates holding pistols to his head.

The pirates are about to kill the Major-General when the police burst out of their hiding places. They struggle, truncheon against sword, but are no match for the agile pirates, who soon stand over them with weapons drawn. "Don't say you're orphans," they snarl, "for we know that game."

But the Sergeant of Police plays his queen: "We charge you yield, in Queen Victoria's name!" And it works. The pirates now kneel while the police stand over them triumphant. "We

The victorious constabulary surround beautiful Mabel.

The Sergeant of Police—whose lot is happier because the pirates love their Queen.

yield at once, with humbled mien,'' says the Pirate King, ''Because, with all our faults, we love our Queen.''

Before the pirates can be taken away for sentencing, Ruth comes forward to stop the police with the astonishing news that these are no common pirates. ''They are all noblemen who have gone wrong!'' To which the Major-General responds:

No Englishman unmoved that statement hears,
Because, with all our faults, we love our House of Peers.
I pray you, pardon me, ex–Pirate King,
Peers will be peers, and youth will have its fling.
Resume your ranks and legislative duties,
And take my daughters, all of whom are beauties.

So all ends merry as a wedding bell, with the Major-General moving among the betrothed couples and conferring his fatherly blessing. The New York premiere, and some more recent productions, have used in place of the traditional reprise of Mabel's ''Poor Wandering One'' a part-reprise of the Major-General's patter song for a finale:

My military knowledge, though I'm plucky and adventury,
Has only been brought down to the beginning of the century.
But still, in getting off my daughters—eight or nine or ten in all,
I've shown myself a model of a modern Major-General.

PATIENCE

OR BUNTHORNE'S BRIDE

The Aesthetic Movement that swept the worlds of art, literature, fashion, and manners in the England of the 1880s was a perfect target for W. S. Gilbert's satiric gibes. In the 1860s Pre-Raphaelite artists and writers like James McNeill Whistler, Edward Burne-Jones, William Morris, and Algernon Swinburne had tried to revolutionize the taste of their philistine society by introducing in their work a graceful romanticism, rich and strange and verging on the erotic. But later disciples, such as young Oscar Wilde, carried the concept to ridiculous extremes. And Gilbert and Sullivan were there to ridicule.

Wilde, a talented undergraduate winner of a poetry prize at Oxford in 1878, often carried or wore a giant sunflower as part of his aesthetic affectation. In *Patience*, Gilbert neatly skewered him and his ilk with the observation that

> *Though the Philistines may jostle, you will rank as an apostle*
> *in the high aesthetic band,*
> *If you walk down Piccadilly with a poppy or a lily*
> *in your mediaeval hand.*

By November, 1880, Gilbert had enough of the "new piece" in hand to want to see Sullivan about it. He had nearly two-thirds of the libretto finished but felt uncomfortable with the premise of two rival clergymen "worshipped by a chorus of female devotees," borrowed from his "The Rival Curates" in *The Bab Ballads*. He fancied instead reverting to his "old idea of rivalry between two aesthetic fanatics . . . I can get much more fun out of the subject as I propose to alter it . . . The Hussars will become aesthetic young men . . . they will all carry lilies in their hands, wear long hair & stained glass attitude."

Patience, "An Entirely New and Original Aesthetic Opera in two acts," opened at the Opéra Comique the following April, and among the author's and composer's fans was none other than Wilde himself. He wrote to George Grossmith, who was playing the poet

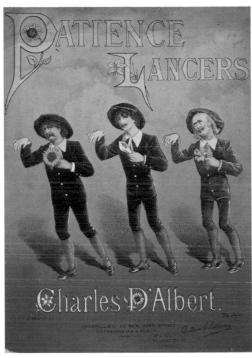

Charles D'Albert arranged Sullivan's opera songs to a variety of dance tempos for Chappell's popular sheet music.

Reginald Bunthorne reads his rapturous poetry to the twenty love-sick maidens.

Bunthorne, asking him to reserve a three-guinea box for him opening night, "if there is one to be had . . . I am looking forward to being greatly amused." The poet Swinburne and artist Whistler—the latter was and remained a friend of Gilbert—were also assumed to be models for the composite portrait of an aesthete in *Patience*. The character's makeup has traditionally followed the Whistler look—long black hair streaked with a lock of white, a languid stance, a small imperial, and a monocle—and then, too, Whistler showed his paintings in the Grosvenor Gallery, which might have given rise to Gilbert's lines "A greenery-yallery, Grosvenor Gallery,/Foot-in-the-grave young man!"

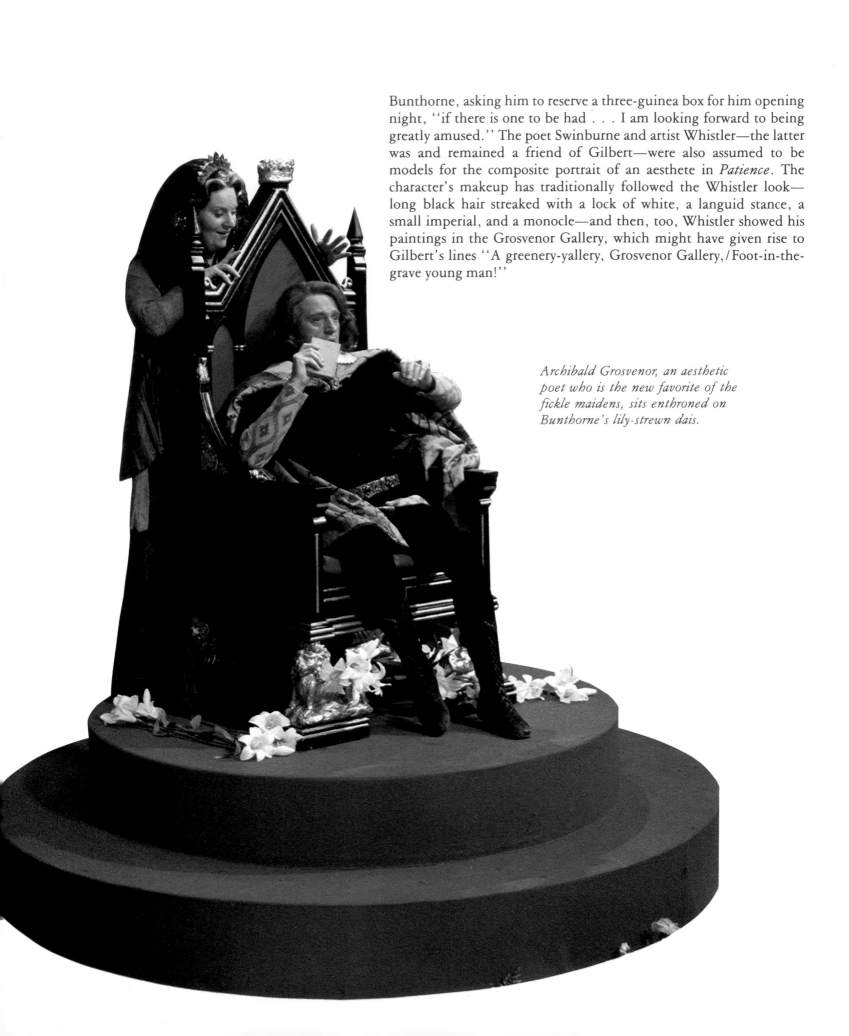

Archibald Grosvenor, an aesthetic poet who is the new favorite of the fickle maidens, sits enthroned on Bunthorne's lily-strewn dais.

In contrast to the two willowy poets, Grosvenor and Bunthorne, there are the Empire-building officers of the 35th Dragoon Guards. In their scarlet jackets and plumed helmets, one would think that they had conquered not only far-flung colonies for the Empire but the heart of every woman back in England. Yet the "twenty love-sick maidens," pining away in pastel draperies, are yearning instead for the velvet-clad poets. It is another of Gilbert's startling paradoxes.

Needless to say, *Patience* was a hit. "Went splendidly," Sullivan noted in his diary. "Eight encores. Seemed a great success." But when the opera opened in New York, business was slack. American audiences who had embraced *Pinafore* and *Pirates* didn't know what to make of this jibe at aestheticism—a cult that had not yet reached their Puritan shores.

D'Oyly Carte, in a brilliant stroke of showmanship, sent Oscar Wilde, the high priest of the aesthetic movement, on a lecture tour all across the United States. The poet came complete with drooping sunflower and velvet suit. Carte also saw to it that Wilde attended a performance of the ailing *Patience* at the Standard Theatre in New York. Wilde's lectures, as well as the opera, profited from the subsequent publicity and Carte reported: "Inscrutable are the ways of the American public and absurd as it may appear, it seems that Oscar Wilde's advent here has caused a regular craze and given the business a fillip up."

But the greatest "fillip up" given to the entire Gilbert and Sullivan business was the building of a large (1,292 seats), modern (the first theater with electric lighting) Savoy Theatre just off the Strand, on the site of John of Gaunt's Savoy Palace. *Patience* opened the theater in October, 1881, with new scenery and costumes worthy of the larger, brighter stage. Sullivan conducted; his friend the Prince of Wales attended; and the *Daily Chronicle* reported next day, "As if by the wave of a fairy's wand," when Carte signaled for the gaslight to be turned down, "the theatre immediately became filled with a soft soothing light, clearer and far more grateful than gas...the audience gave a cheer."

Thus, *Patience* became the first "Savoy" opera, as well as breaking all previous records with an initial run of 578 performances. And a new word, Savoyard, would be taken into the language for devotees and performers of Gilbert and Sullivan comic operas.

Lady Jane, an oversized, overage maiden mad about the poet, is about to draw a ticket in a raffle for Bunthorne's fair hand.

PATIENCE

OR BUNTHORNE'S BRIDE

ACT I: *Exterior of Castle Bunthorne.*

IN THE GARDENS BEFORE CASTLE BUNTHORNE a group of young ladies in the last stages of despair are mooning about, plucking on lutes and mandolins and singing sad songs of unrequited love:

> *Twenty love-sick maidens we,*
>> *Love-sick all against our will.*
> *Twenty years hence we shall be*
>> *Twenty love-sick maidens still. . . .*
>
> *All our love is all for one,*
>> *Yet that love he heedeth not.*
> *He is coy and cares for none,*
>> *Sad and sorry is our lot!*

The maids are dressed in aesthetic draperies—no stylish corsets or wasp waists for them! Gilbert himself had designed the costumes, which were made of fabrics from Liberty and Company in the murky colors beloved by the Pre-Raphaelites.

The well-born ladies are in raptures over Reginald Bunthorne, a poet and aesthete who is icily insensible of their affections, and his indifference to them all is what binds them to one another. "The love of maidens is, to him, as interesting as the taxes!" pouts Lady Ella. "Would that it were," Lady Saphir at once retorts. "He pays his taxes!"

But Lady Jane, an elderly spinster of heroic proportions, who is also mad about the poet, has unpleasant news. Bunthorne may be indifferent to all of them, but he does love, wildly. His weird fancy has lighted on none other than Patience, the village milkmaid. Just yesterday he was caught by Lady Jane in the girl's dairy sinfully "eating fresh butter with a tablespoon."

While this is sinking in, Patience herself makes an appearance, a charming young eighteenth-century Dresden china figurine in tight-

Dramatis Personae:

COLONEL CALVERLEY (Baritone)
MAJOR MURGATROYD (Baritone) — Officers of Dragoon Guards
LIEUT. THE DUKE OF DUNSTABLE (Tenor)

REGINALD BUNTHORNE, a Fleshly Poet (Baritone)

ARCHIBALD GROSVENOR, an Idyllic P (Baritone)

MR. BUNTHORNE'S SOLICITOR

THE LADY ANGELA (Mezzo-soprano)
THE LADY SAPHIR (Mezzo-soprano) — Rapturous Maidens
THE LADY ELLA (Soprano)
THE LADY JANE (Contralto)

PATIENCE, a Dairy Maid (Soprano)

Chorus of Rapturous Maidens and Officers of Dragoon Guards

First produced at the Opéra Comique on April 23, 1881.

"Love feeds on hope, they say, or love will die . . .
Yet my love lives, although no hope have I!"

ly laced bodice, ruffled neckline, and saucy skirts. She is totally innocent of love, never having experienced it, and looking around at the other maids' unhappiness, she's rather glad she hasn't.

Thinking to cheer them up, Patience gives them some good news—the 35th Dragoon Guards have returned to the village and are on their way to this very spot now. "We care nothing for Dragoon Guards!" says one young woman with disdain.

"But, bless me, you were all engaged to them a year ago!" exclaims Patience, who really cannot understand what love is all about, even when it is explained to her that the ladies' tastes have been "etherealized," their perceptions "exalted" in this year. Off they go to serenade their poet on lutes and mandolins, while Patience looks after them in utter astonishment.

And now the soft colors and tender melancholy songs of the maidens, their languid attitudinizing, is brusquely replaced by the corps of Dragoon Guards, who march in with a smart flourish, a stirring sight in their brilliant scarlet coats, high boots, and gold braid. "The soldiers of our Queen/Are linked in friendly tether," they boom cheerfully, having come to call upon the ladies, whom they have not seen for nearly a year. They obviously feel themselves irresistible to friend and foe alike, and Colonel Calverley, fairly bursting with military fervor, reels off a recipe for "that popular mystery/Known to the world as a Heavy Dragoon." It is another Gilbertian tour de force, a patter song that requires an imposing actor with a big voice and commanding personality, and then it's easy:

> Take all the remarkable people in history,
>   Rattle them off to a popular tune.

Starting with Lord Nelson, adding a mixed bag of great and colorful people like Bismarck, Fielding, Macaulay, Dickens, Thackeray, Thomas Aquinas, and Madame Tussaud, among a host of other famous and obscure names that are ingeniously linked and rhymed, the Colonel directs that they all be melted down in a crucible; then:

> Set them to simmer and take off the scum,
>   And a Heavy Dragoon is the residuum!

His fellow officers are in complete and immodest agreement.

The dragoons spy their ladies coming across the lawn. "But who is the gentleman with the long hair?" they wonder. "He seems popular." Of course, it is Bunthorne the poet, in the throes of composing a poem. The ladies all kneel to him, but he has eyes only for Patience. He recites his "wild, weird, fleshly" poem for her, and wanders off to write some more. While the ladies find it "fragrant" and "precious," Patience admits honestly that the poem seems to her to be nonsense.

The Colonel and his men have had enough, and they remind the ladies that they are engaged to them. But the ladies are appalled

Bunthorne, in Patience's dairy, sinfully gorging on fresh butter with a tablespoon.

Patience tells the despondent maidens that she has never loved and, therefore, unlike them she is "blithe and gay."

at the unaesthetic dragoons. Lady Jane points to their uniforms. "Red and yellow! Primary colours!" she exclaims in horror, and the ladies drift off two by two singing their lovesick lament while their erstwhile fiancés look after them in chagrined astonishment.

The Colonel cannot stand this insult to the British uniform "that has been as successful in the courts of Venus as on the field of Mars!" He is amazed and angry that the dragoon uniform no longer seems to work its amatory magic on young beauties, and complains:

> *But the peripatetics*
> *Of long-haired aesthetics*
> *Are very much more to their taste—*

And the dragoons stomp off in high dudgeon as well as in the high black boots that used to be considered so devastatingly attractive.

Bunthorne, alone and unobserved, drops his pose, admitting that he is an "aesthetic sham":

> *Let me confess!*
> *A languid love for lilies does* not *blight me! . . .*
>
> *I am* not *fond of uttering platitudes*
> *In stained-glass attitudes.*
> *In short, my mediaevalism's affectation,*
> *Born of a morbid love of admiration!*

He then sings a brilliant "point patter," a patter song taken at less than breakneck speed in order to make clear the important sentiments listed—in this case, what is needed "to shine in the high aesthetic line as a man of culture rare." If one of the requirements is a "vegetable love," of lilies or sunflowers, for example, then that would not suit Bunthorne. For here comes Patience, and he loves her. In fact, he even offers to cut off his hair if she would like him to.

But Patience, who knows nothing of love, having never loved but her great-aunt, says she's quite sure she could never love Bunthorne. Brokenhearted and desolate, Bunthorne takes his leave. Patience, puzzling over this mysterious thing called love, is troubled until she sees Lady Angela and asks her about it: ". . . how is it to be distinguished from insanity?"

Lady Angela tells her it is "the one unselfish emotion," and Patience determines to fall head over heels with *somebody* rather than risk being selfish. The only experience of love she might have had, she recalls, was when she was a babe of four and played with another child—a little boy "of beauty rare." But, "Pray don't misconstrue," she tells Angela. "Remember . . . He was a *little* boy!" And the more worldly Angela responds, "The interesting fact remains—/He was a little *boy*!"

At this point, enter Grosvenor, the "Idyllic Poet," rival of Bunthorne in literary style and, as it immediately transpires, in love as

"*The soldiers of our Queen*
Are linked in friendly tether;
Upon the battle scene
They fight the foe together."

Grosvenor, the Idyllic Poet,
asks: "Prithee, pretty
maiden—prithee, tell me true,
(Hey, but I'm doleful,
willow willow waly)
Have you e'er a lover
a-dangling after you?"

well. He wastes no time, courting Patience in a charming duet with eighteenth-century overtones in its "Hey willow waly O!" refrain. (Audiences left the theater delightedly repeating, "Hey willow waly O!" though nobody knew exactly what it meant.)

In spite of the catchy allure of his song, Patience will not marry Grosvenor because she doesn't know him. But wonder of wonders! Grosvenor turns out to be her little playfellow, Archibald.

A cross Archibald must bear is his unrivaled beauty, which causes him to be "madly loved at first sight" by every woman he meets. He cannot follow Patience's suggestion and disfigure himself, for he is "a trustee for Beauty" and has an obligation to fulfill. He is also called "Archibald the All-Right" because he is infallible.

Patience is now marvelously happy. She knows what love is at last. It is Archibald Grosvenor!

But horrors! If he is perfection, and "a source of endless ecstasy," then there can be nothing unselfish in loving him. So, tragically, they must part. Patience's sorrow is short-lived, however, for since she is "plain, homely, unattractive" she realizes that the love of a man like Grosvenor for a girl like her would perforce be unselfishness itself. He may continue loving her, then, though they cannot wed.

Act I ends in a glorious finale. Bunthorne is led in, rose-crowned, hung about with garlands, and looking very miserable as might befit a sacrificial offering. He is led by two of the maidens and accompanied by a procession of the others, dancing classically and playing on cymbals, double pipes, and other archaic instruments.

Despairing of Patience's love, Bunthorne, on the advice of his Solicitor, has put himself up to be raffled. Money to go to charity, Bunthorne to go as husband to the winner. This turn of plot most probably was carried over from Gilbert's earlier concept dealing with rival curates rather than poets. As a satirization of popular church lotteries it would have been doubly funny.

When the dragoons march in and see what's up, they curse the Solicitor and implore the maidens on bended knee (that never bent "to foemen's steel") not to abandon the men to whom they are plighted. Bunthorne's patience is wearing thin, and to speed up the raffle he resorts to a bit of high-pressure shilling:

> *Come, walk up, and purchase with avidity,*
> *Overcome your diffidence and natural timidity,*
> *Tickets for the raffle should be purchased with avidity,*
> *Put in half a guinea and a husband you may gain—*

Just as Lady Jane is about to reach into the bowl to draw her ticket, Patience enters and stops her. The milkmaid will marry Bunthorne after all, since loving him would be the height of unselfishness. And off they go together, hand in hand.

At that, the Dragoon Guards suddenly appear very attractive to the maidens, who remember the "soft note of the echoing voice / Of

Patience interrupts Bunthorne's raffle to offer herself unselfishly as his bride.

"How rapturously these maidens love me, and how hopelessly! Oh, Patience, Patience . . ." murmurs the beleaguered Grosvenor.

Lady Jane laments how sad "that woman's lot who, year by year, / Sees, one by one, her beauties disappear . . ."

an old, old love." Each girl embraces her dragoon, Patience and Bunthorne return, everything seems happily sorted out, when—beautiful Grosvenor strolls by, immersed in the book he is reading. He takes no notice of the others, but the maidens are strangely fascinated by this new and very graceful poet.

Little by little they move away from their dragoons, and when they discover that Grosvenor, too, is an aesthetic they kneel around him. The Dragoon Guards are horrified; Bunthorne and Patience are horrified; Grosvenor himself is triple-horrified. Bunthorne is so envious that he throws a small daisy in his rival's face; Patience is about to attack the maidens in a frenzy of jealousy; Grosvenor inveighs against his "cursed comeliness." The dragoons, however, have the last word, a rousing reprise of their song upon first discovering their ladies' unbelievable attachment to a literary man:

> *Now is not this ridiculous—and is not this preposterous?*
> *A thorough-paced absurdity—explain it if you can.*

ACT II: *A glade.*

IN A GREEN GLADE THE ELDERLY LADY JANE IS DISCOVERED leaning upon a violoncello, with which she presently accompanies herself. She alone has remained loyal to Bunthorne and hopes, since her charms are already "ripe" if not "decaying," that he will soon abandon the milkmaid for her.

The other maidens are once again sick with hopeless love of a poet—this time it is Grosvenor at whose feet they worship. His thoughts are of Patience, and desperate to escape his adoring followers he reads and sings to them several truly atrocious poems, including "A Magnet Hung in a Hardware Shop." This last seems sufficiently depressing to cause the maidens to drift away with sad backward looks from time to time. "A curse on my fatal beauty," sighs Grosvenor, "for I am sick of conquests!"

Patience has managed to slip away from Bunthorne in order to ask Grosvenor if he still loves her. In the course of their conversation—during which Grosvenor tries to hold her hand or come closer and is always conscientiously repulsed—Patience lets him know that she doesn't really love Bunthorne and is only acting out of a sense of duty, but she must stay with the man she's promised to. Grosvenor gazes at her sorrowfully and takes his leave, at which Patience bursts into tears.

When Bunthorne and Lady Jane come upon the weeping dairymaid, Bunthorne is angered to discover that Patience thinks "dear Archibald" is "the noblest, purest, and most perfect being I have ever met." Snapping his fingers in her face, he stalks off, with Lady Jane in hot pursuit. He is furious that his "love-sick maidens" all follow Grosvenor now, and resolves to confront the poet and de-

"A curse on my fatal beauty, for I am sick of conquests!"

*"You hold yourself like this (attitude),
You hold yourself like that (attitude),
By hook and crook you try to look
    both angular and flat (attitude)."*

mand that he abandon aestheticism—there is room for only one aesthete in the county.

However, the field is going to be more crowded than Bunthorne could have imagined. For Colonel Calverley, Major Murgatroyd, and the Duke of Dunstable have traded in their dragoon uniforms for aesthetic garb; they are carrying a sunflower, a poppy, and an orchid, respectively. They now have long hair, and are attempting to strike the stained-glass attitudes—in gross exaggeration—adopted by Bunthorne and his maidens earlier. The effect is even more ludicrous since the three officers tend to strike their languid poses with military precision. When Saphir and Angela see them, they cry, "How Botticellian!" finding them "consummately utter." And the two agree that if Grosvenor should not choose either of them, their yearning hearts will go out to the aestheticized soldiers instead.

Bunthorne and Grosvenor at last come face-to-face for their showdown. Bunthorne, who cannot live without admiration, threatens his rival with a terrible curse if Grosvenor refuses to make a complete change at once. "You must cut your hair...In appearance and costume you must be absolutely commonplace," he orders.

Grosvenor finally yields, and is even cheerful, having long wished for just such a reasonable pretext to make the change. "I do it on compulsion!" he says gratefully. The two poets then sing a duet in which Bunthorne lists his aesthetic attributes while Grosvenor paints a self-portrait of the commonplace young man he will become:

Aestheticism has been discarded and the dragoons are once again in military uniform; the maidens have become "pattering," "chattering," "every-day young girls."

> GROS. *An every-day young man:*
> *A commonplace type,*
> *With a stick and a pipe,*
> *And a half-bred black-and-tan ...*
>
> BUN. *A pallid and thin young man,*
> *A haggard and lank young man,*
> *A greenery-yallery, Grosvenor Gallery,*
> *Foot-in-the-grave young man!*

And now Bunthorne, too, is a changed character, giving up his ill nature for the cheerfulness that was one of his rival poet's charms. As he dances about the stage humming a song, Patience comes upon him with astonishment. When she discovers how amiable Bunthorne has grown, she throws herself into his arms. "It will no longer be a duty to love you, but a pleasure—a rapture—an ecstasy!" she exclaims. Then, realizing that there can be nothing unselfish in loving so perfect a being as Bunthorne has now become, she renounces him.

At this moment the stage is thronged with a cheerful group of young ladies who have exchanged their draperies for tennis frocks, riding habits, even Scottish Highland dress. They are following Grosvenor, who is wearing a business suit, his short hair covered by a bowler hat. Last of all, in come the splendidly martial Dragoon Guards.

Plain Jane, who was almost Bunthorne's bride, leaps at the chance to become a duchess instead.

When Patience sees commonplace Grosvenor she realizes she is now free to love this imperfect specimen, and they embrace. Bunthorne is crushed, but loyal Lady Jane cheers him up: "I have never left you, and I never will!" But wait! The Duke of Dunstable has finally determined to take a bride. In common fairness he has decided to take the only maiden who has "the misfortune to be distinctly plain." Jane!

For the chance to be a duchess, faithful Jane leaves Bunthorne's side in a twinkling. Everyone else pairs off, leaving only Bunthorne partnerless. As for the poet:

> *He will have to be contented*
> *With a tulip or lily! . . .*
>
> *Greatly pleased with one another,*
> *To get married we decide.*
> *Each of us will wed the other,*
> *Nobody be Bunthorne's Bride!*

So ends *Patience*, or *Bunthorne's Bride*, Gilbert's typical little joke wherein, title to the contrary, Patience is not the opera's leading character, nor does Bunthorne get a bride.

IOLANTHE

OR THE PEER AND THE PERI

Less than a fortnight after *Patience* opened the Savoy Theatre, Gilbert called on Sullivan with a rough idea for their next opera. "Lord Chancellor . . . Peers, Fairies, etc," Sullivan noted in his diary; "funny, but at present vague."

Obviously Gilbert had to try to catch his collaborator when he could, for Sullivan was a stylish gypsy, traipsing to Denmark, Russia, Germany, and Egypt in the exalted company of royalty and not very easy to pin down to the lucrative but less than illustrious job of setting the music for a comic opera. Yet it was the considerable money pouring in from these operas that allowed Sullivan to move in high circles, and both men to live lavishly. Gilbert was all for perpetuating the creative partnership, and so he was hard at work on the next libretto while Carte basked in the electric limelight of the new Savoy Theatre and Sullivan was traveling in high style.

Once again Gilbert turned to the supernatural for inspiration. This time his libretto told of "a fairy/Light and airy/Married with a mortal." Their child was an "Arcadian Shepherd," who became a peer. The House of Lords, the upper House of Parliament where the peers of the realm carried on their deliberations (when they deigned to attend), presided over by the Lord Chancellor, was a gold mine of comedic and satirical possibilities. Gilbert took full advantage of the controversy surrounding the hereditary nature of the House of Lords: ". . . with a House of Peers composed exclusively of people of intellect, what's to become of the House of Commons?" asks a querulous and not very bright hereditary earl. Somehow, set to Sullivan's delightfully melodic music, the sting was removed from Gilbert's jibes and the public roared with laughter.

The first-night audience sparkled with luminaries, including the Prince of Wales and Prime Minister Gladstone, whose Liberal Party traditionally campaigned against the House of Lords. (Gladstone's annual salary was said to be less than the earnings of either Gilbert or

"Tripping hither, tripping thither,
Nobody knows why or whither;
We must dance and we must sing
Round about our fairy ring!"

Magnificent in their red velvet and ermine ceremonial robes, the peers
swagger into the House of Lords.

IOLANTHE 115

Sullivan!) The innovative electric lighting of the theater and stage was augmented by an additional electric novelty dreamed up by Gilbert. The fairies carried wands and wore little stars in their hair that lighted up and flickered about on the darkened stage, bringing gasps of amazement from the sophisticated audience.

The road to this triumph had been a rocky one. For Sullivan it was, as he noted in his diary, ''The dark year.'' His beloved mother had died on June 1. Two days later, ''music, that most brutal of all mistresses,'' as he once called it, took him in hand as he began work

Strephon is comforted by his fairy mother, Iolanthe, whose supernatural youthfulness arouses suspicion.

on the score for *Iolanthe*. He would compose all night and then scrap most of the music in the morning. Progress was snail-paced.

There was also the constant threat of pirates in the United States, where the popular *Patience* was subject to many infringements that earned not a cent for the three partners. To foil the pirates this time, the new opera was being called *Perola* while in rehearsal, and a dual opening was planned for New York and London.

Three weeks before *Iolanthe* was scheduled to open on both sides of the Atlantic, the composer was still struggling through the night to write a new duet, the Overture remained to be written, and there were final rehearsals to be directed. Then, just as he was leaving for the Savoy to conduct the opening-night performance, Sullivan received a note advising him that his broker had gone bankrupt, wiping out his savings of £7,000. Furthermore, early in the run, his fur-lined overcoat would be stolen from the theater's green room! Well, *Iolanthe* was a success, Gilbert and Sullivan were heartily cheered, but the composer's diary notes, "Very low afterwards. Came home."

After that there was nowhere to go but up. Sullivan got his coat back within a week; the opera was a great success in the United States as well as in England, where it ran for fourteen months, recouping Sullivan's fortunes; he was knighted at Windsor Castle by Queen Victoria six months later; and Gilbert, as always eager to get on with it, began drafting the plot of the next opera—which he was to submit for his collaborator's approval before the year was over.

"The constitutional guardian I Of pretty young Wards in Chancery . . ."

IOLANTHE

OR THE PEER AND THE PERI

ACT I: *An Arcadian landscape.*

WE ARE IN AN ARCADIAN LANDSCAPE bordered by a little river that is crossed by a rustic bridge. A chorus of dainty fairies led by Leila, Celia, and Fleta dance in, "Tripping hither, tripping thither," round about their fairy ring. But their revels are not what they used to be, they lament, since Iolanthe, the beloved "life and soul of Fairyland," was banished twenty-five years ago for marrying a mortal.

Actually, Iolanthe's offense had merited the death penalty, but the Fairy Queen, who loved her, too, commuted her sentence to penal servitude for life at the bottom of a nearby pond. The fairies beg their queen to forgive Iolanthe and bring her back to them because they love and miss her so. The Queen shares their feelings, for: "Who taught me to curl myself inside a buttercup? . . . Who taught me to swing upon a cobweb? . . . to dive into a dewdrop—to nestle in a nutshell—to gambol upon gossamer? Iolanthe!" (Shades of Mercutio's Queen Mab speech in Shakespeare's *Romeo and Juliet.*) Since the Fairy Queen is a female of Wagnerian proportions, dressed somewhat like Brunnhilde, this passage, though played straight, elicits laughter.

Iolanthe is summoned and rises from the water, still a beautiful seventeen-year-old, clad in waterweeds that fall from her when she is pardoned and are replaced by fairy garments and a diamond coronet. She tells the assembled fairies that she is the mother of a twenty-four-year-old son, Strephon, who loves Phyllis, a Ward in Chancery. Strephon is a fairy down to the waist, but his legs are mortal, and neither he nor his father know about one another. The fairies, naturally, are very curious to see this creature. They have not long to wait.

Strephon, an Arcadian shepherd, now enters, singing, dancing, and tootling prettily on a flageolet. He greets his mother with the happy announcement that he is to be married to Phyllis that very

Dramatis Personae:

THE LORD CHANCELLOR (Baritone)

EARL OF MOUNTARARAT (Baritone)

EARL TOLLOLLER (Tenor)

PRIVATE WILLIS, of the Grenadier Guards (Bass-baritone)

STREPHON, an Arcadian Shepherd (Baritone)

QUEEN OF THE FAIRIES (Contralto)

IOLANTHE, a Fairy, Strephon's Mother (Mezzo-soprano)

CELIA (Soprano)
LEILA (Mezzo-soprano) } Fairies
FLETA (Soprano)

PHYLLIS, an Arcadian Shepherdess and Ward in Chancery (Soprano)

Chorus of Dukes, Marquises, Earls, Viscounts, Barons, and Fairies

First produced at the Savoy Theatre, London, November 25, 1882. Simultaneous production at the Standard Theatre, New York.

"The feelings of a Lord Chancellor who is in love with a Ward of Court are not to be envied."

day, in spite of the fact that her guardian, the powerful Lord Chancellor, has not given his permission. He has not told Phyllis of his fairy ancestry lest it frighten her. "My brain is a fairy brain," he explains to his mother and the other peris, "but from the waist downwards I'm a gibbering idiot."

The Queen has an idea. With his fairy brain she believes he would do well in an intellectual sphere, and she offers him a borough that would give him a seat in Parliament. But Strephon isn't sure. The fairies take their leave after telling him to call on them if he ever needs help and they will come at once.

Strephon is joined by Phyllis, a delectable Arcadian shepherdess, and the two lovers sing a most tender duet, their soprano and baritone backed by quavering strings that invest Gilbert's words and Sullivan's music with warmth and feeling:

> *None shall part us from each other,*
> *One in life and death are we:*
> *All in all to one another—*
> *I to thee and thou to me!*
>
> *Thou the tree and I the flower—*
> *Thou the idol; I the throng—*
> *Thou the day and I the hour—*
> *Thou the singer; I the song!*

Strephon insists that they must marry at once, even without the Lord Chancellor's permission, because with half the House of Lords sighing at Phyllis's feet, he might lose her if they wait. She might even fall in love with the Lord Chancellor himself! "Yes," Phyllis agrees, she might. "He's a clean old gentleman." So they decide that delays are dangerous and, loving each other as they do, they had better marry, the sooner the better. And off they go.

Now, on the empty stage, the most gorgeous spectacle of any of the Gilbert and Sullivan operas takes place. Gilbert's words and staging are wedded with the greatest theatricality to Sullivan's triumphal music. To create the properly realistic setting for Gilbert's spoof of parliamentary high jinks that is to follow, it is first necessary to render the scene with utmost fidelity. The fairies are creatures of the imagination, but the peers must be presented as they actually are.

On opening night and at several special performances, on marched the actual Grenadier Guards in full scarlet uniforms with tall black busbys. Following them were the peers, who, in Gilbert's directions were to march "with great state in single rank and somewhat swaggering gesture." The peers were magnificent in their ceremonial robes—yards of red velvet, ermine capelets, gold and jeweled insignia of the high orders of knighthood—Garter, Bath, St. Patrick, Thistle—with the proper coronets, gold balls, and leaves appropriate to each. So that everything would be totally correct and realistic, the robes were replicas made by Queen Victoria's own court robe makers, Messrs. Ede & Son. "For heaven's sake," a concerned Gilbert snapped at his Lords during the dress rehearsal, "wear your

"Iolanthe!
From thy dark exile thou art summoned!
Come to our call—
Come, Iolanthe!"

"Fare thee well, attractive stranger.
Shouldst thou be in doubt or danger,
Peril or perplexitee,
Call us, and we'll come to thee!"

The troubled lovers, Strephon and Phyllis, with a sympathetic Iolanthe.

coronets as though you were used to them.''

Gilbert and Sullivan gave the chorus an exhilarating song whose words and music resound with brassy, class-conscious hubris:

> *Loudly let the trumpet bray!*
> > *Tantantara!*
> > *Proudly bang the sounding brasses!*
> > *Tzing! Boom! . . .*
>
> *Bow, bow, ye lower middle classes!*
> *Bow, bow, ye tradesmen, bow, ye masses!*
> *Blow the trumpets, bang the brasses!*
> > *Tantantara! Tzing! Boom!*
> *We are peers of highest station,*
> *Paragons of legislation,*
> *Pillars of the British nation!*
> > *Tantantara! Tzing! Boom!*

It was—and is—a striking moment in the theater, for all its mock-heroic humor.

The Lord Chancellor, wearing a full-bottomed wig and his black velvet and gold robes of office, followed by his little train-bearer, enters last. As head of the House of Lords and its chief judicial officer, he is one of the loftiest and most powerful personages in the realm.

The Woolsack, the seat from which he presides, is second only to the throne as a seat of power. Gilbert is taking on a giant!

Since the Lords would ordinarily appear in all their splendor only on the greatest occasions of state, British audiences would, naturally, understand the exaggerated humor of this gorgeous stage procession. Gilbert, however, wondered mischievously whether their American friends, seeing the New York production, would imagine ''that British lords are to be seen walking about our streets garbed in this fashion.''

The Lord Chancellor's song, first delivered by George Grossmith, is another of Gilbert's brilliant irreverences:

> *The Law is the true embodiment*
> *Of everything that's excellent.*
> *It has no kind of fault or flaw,*
> *And I, my Lords, embody the Law. . . .*
>
> *And every one who'd marry a Ward*
> *Must come to me for my accord,*
> *And in my court I sit all day,*
> *Giving agreeable girls away . . . .*
> *   Which is exasperating for*
> *   A highly susceptible Chancellor!*

'' 'Tis I—young Strephon—mine this priceless treasure!
    Against the world I claim my darling's hand!''

And now the House of Lords gets down to the important business of the day. Namely, that all the peers are suitors of Phyllis, while the susceptible Lord Chancellor, who is also in love with the girl but can't award her to himself, will have to approve her choice. ''Ah, my Lords, it is indeed painful,'' he laments, ''to have to sit upon a woolsack which is stuffed with such thorns as these!''

''Phyllis . . . has so powerfully affected your Lordships, that you have appealed to me . . . to give her to whichever one of you she may think proper to select . . .''

"Why you want us we don't know,
But you've summoned us, and so
Enter all the little fairies . . ."

When Phyllis appears before the Bar she admits her heart is given to another. Earl Tolloller begs her not to spurn those who are nobly born—"Hearts just as pure and fair/May beat in Belgrave Square." But when Strephon comes to claim his darling's hand, the Lord Chancellor denies them permission to wed. He turns a deaf ear to Strephon's pleas on the grounds that his duty to the law forbids him to let them wed and, before he sweeps out of the chamber, he imparts his witty formula for a successful career in the law: "When I went to the Bar as a very young man, (Said I to myself—said I) . . .' '

Strephon is heartbroken, but his mother comes to comfort him. She tells him that he can defy the Lord Chancellor's power, since he is half a fairy—"down to the waist." Iolanthe will take his case to the Queen of the Fairies, who has promised her protection.

Unobserved by mother and son, the peers tiptoe into the back of the chamber with Phyllis. They see Strephon being consoled by a beautiful young girl, and Phyllis accuses him of being unfaithful. Neither she nor the peers will believe that Iolanthe is his mother, and Phyllis, in a fit of pique, says she will marry one of the peers—she doesn't care which one. "I'll be a countess, shall I not?"

In despair, Strephon calls on his fairy aunts, who come tripping in. The Fairy Queen tells the Lord Chancellor, who has returned, that he's done the shepherd an injustice, "for the lady *is* his mother." To which the Chancellor replies that he "didn't see her face, but if they fondled one another,/And she's but seventeen—I don't believe it was his mother!/Taradiddle, taradiddle./Tol lol lay!"

The Queen is so angry at being treated high-handedly that she casts a powerful spell. Strephon is to throw away his shepherd's crook and ribbons and go into Parliament:

Every bill and every measure
That may gratify his pleasure,
Though your fury it arouses,
Shall be passed by both your Houses!

Perhaps most terrible of all:

You shall sit, if he sees reason,
Through the grouse and salmon season . . .

"No!" the peers cry from the heart.

As the curtain falls, the Lords fall to their knees begging for mercy. Phyllis implores Strephon to relent but he refuses.

ACT II: *Palace Yard, Westminster.*

THE PALACE YARD BY MOONLIGHT, bounded on one side by part of the old medieval Palace of Westminster and at the rear by the tower of Big Ben, is an impressive scene. Private Willis stands guard, in his scarlet grenadier uniform with tall black busby, shouldering a rifle with a long bayonet. He has a big, deep voice and sings a song about the British party system, its Liberals and Conservatives.

The fairies enter and dance about, delighted at Strephon's impact on Parliament.

To his measures all assent—
Showing that fairies have their uses. . . .

Lords and Commons are both in the blues!
Strephon makes them shake in their shoes!

Phyllis, believing her simple swain is untrue, says she will now choose one of the Lords—"and I don't care which!"

The Queen of the Fairies admits she is not insensible to the effect of Sentry Willis's manly beauty. "Look at that man! A perfect picture!"

The angered peers stamp out after a late night session of the House of Lords, where Strephon has a bill up "to throw the Peerage open to Competitive Examination!" They glower at the fairies, and Lord Mountararat snarls, "This comes of women interfering in politics"—a line that brings down the house in these times more thunderously than when prime ministers were exclusively men.

The fairies have grown increasingly fond of the peers and, while they seem to be at cross-purposes with the noblemen and will not stop their protégé Strephon, their song is ambivalent as the peers are leaving:

> *We're very cross indeed—*
> *Yes, very cross,*
> *Don't go!*

They gaze wistfully after the departing Lord Montararat and Earl Tolloller and are caught in the act by the Fairy Queen, who reminds them that it is death to marry a mortal. "Yes, but it's not death to *wish* to marry a mortal!" responds sensible Leila.

The Queen, too, is susceptible to male beauty and finds herself drawn to Private Willis: "You're a very fine fellow, sir," she says. "I am generally admired," he replies truthfully. The fairies sing of the fires of love that glow "with heat intense" and can be extinguished only by "the hose of common sense." And then they apostrophize Captain Shaw, who was chief of London's Metropolitan Fire Brigade at that time:

> *Could thy Brigade*
> *With cold cascade*
> *Quench my great love, I wonder!*

The Captain was in the star-studded Savoy Theatre for *Iolanthe*'s opening, and the song made quite a stir at the time.

Love is faring badly with everyone. Phyllis is engaged to two noblemen at once and she is miserable. The Lord Chancellor has insomnia because of the agonies of his unrequited love for Phyllis, and he staggers out to deliver a long, fast, nonstop patter song (known as "the nightmare song") that is probably a nightmare for the nimble-tongued performer who has to sing it. It begins calmly enough:

> *When you're lying awake with a dismal headache, and repose is taboo'd by anxiety . . .*

But after thirty-odd long, tightly packed lines, with internal rhymes and a galloping meter, the Lord Chancellor is hard put to come up with another dozen lines as encore.

Earl Tolloller and Lord Mountararat, distressed to see their leader in so pitiable a condition, sing the Lord Chancellor a pep song crammed with about a dozen inspirational proverbs, exhorting him to "go in" and press his suit with the lady. This trio of Lord Chancellor and two peers cavorting about, and ending with the Lord

Chancellor twirling into Private Willis's sentry box to escape the audience's clamor for still another encore, is one of the high points of the opera. The three dignitaries dance off together arm-in-arm.

Strephon arrives on the scene in obvious low spirits in spite of his successful leadership of both parties in Parliament. He yearns for Phyllis, and when she appears he discloses the truth—that his mother is a fairy, making him half a fairy, but only half a mortal. "I'd rather have half a mortal I do love, than half a dozen I don't!" is Phyllis's smart rejoinder through her tears, and she pleads with Strephon to forgive her.

When Strephon explains that not only his mother but all his fairy aunts look like young girls, Phyllis agrees that whenever she sees him kissing a very young lady she'll know it's only "an elderly relative." So they decide to marry, and soon. "We might change our minds," says Strephon. "We'll get married first." "And change our minds afterwards?" Phyllis asks. "That's the usual course," Strephon replies.

When Iolanthe joins them, they tell her the good news and ask her, with her fairy eloquence, to plead their case with the Lord Chancellor. But Iolanthe refuses, finally admitting that it is none other than the Lord Chancellor who is her husband and Strephon's father. She may not reveal her identity to him, under penalty of death, as he believes her to have died, childless.

Iolanthe raises her veil and reveals herself to the Lord Chancellor as his wife, an act that dooms her to die.

"Soon as we may,
Off and away!
We'll commence our journey airy—
Happy are we—
As you can see,
Every one is now a fairy!"

As she sees the gentleman in question approaching, she quickly veils herself while the young couple tiptoe away. When her moving plea in behalf of Strephon is denied by the Lord Chancellor, Iolanthe is forced to break her vow and reveal herself as his wife and the mother of their son.

At this there is a chorus of wails from the fairies, offstage— "Aiaiah! Aiaiah! . . . Willaloo!" suggestive of the Rhine Maidens in *Das Rheingold*—author and composer having a little more fun with Richard Wagner! The Fairy Queen and her fairies now appear and the Queen, raising her spear, is about to plunge it into Iolanthe's breast.

As the peers and Private Willis join the others, Leila stops the Queen, telling her that she would have to kill all the fairies, for all have sinned—they have become "fairy duchesses, marchionesses, countesses, viscountesses, and baronesses." The peers take the blame for being so irresistible, explaining, "They couldn't help themselves." "It seems they *have* helped themselves, and pretty freely, too!" snaps the Queen.

She unrolls a scroll on which the law clearly states that every fairy must die who marries a mortal. But the Lord Chancellor, who didn't arrive at the top of the judicial heap for nothing, solves the dilemma neatly. Looking over the document, he sees that the simple insertion of one word would solve everything and the Queen alters her scroll accordingly in pencil, to: "Every fairy shall die who *doesn't* marry a mortal."

But now *her* life is in jeopardy, so she calls Private Willis forward and asks if he will save a lady in distress and become a "fairy guardsman." The moment he agrees, wings sprout from his shoulders.

The peers decide that now that the House of Lords is to recruit its members "entirely from persons of intelligence," there's not much use in their staying down here. Wings spring from the shoulders of the peers, and away they all fly to Fairyland, singing:

Up in the sky,
Ever so high,
Pleasures come in endless series;
We will arrange
Happy exchange—
House of Peers for House of Peris!

PRINCESS IDA
BY W.S.GILBERT AND ARTHUR SULLIVAN
Grand Theatre,
LEEDS,
Monday, Sept. 19th.

Clement-Smith & Co. Lith
317 Strand London

PRINCESS IDA

OR CASTLE ADAMANT

Having satirized Oscar Wilde and the aesthetic movement in *Patience*, and the House of Lords in *Iolanthe*, Gilbert's jaundiced eye now lit upon the emancipation of women as a theme worthy of his barbed wit. He quite agreed with the son of that remarkable and powerful woman ruler of Great Britain, the Prince of Wales, who had "no sympathy at all" for suffragettes and believed that higher education for females was "absurd."

Fourteen years earlier Gilbert had written a play inspired by Alfred, Lord Tennyson's poem *The Princess*, with its "sweet girl-graduates in their golden hair." He called his play "a respectful perversion" of the poem, and in it he lambasted feminists and women who thought that females had an aptitude for higher education—all in blank verse. He now took over his old play almost lock, stock, and barrel, keeping much of the dialogue and blank-verse form, and turned it into *Princess Ida*, "a respectful Operatic Perversion of Tennyson's *Princess*."

Iolanthe's reviews had been mixed, and in case its run would not come up to expectations, Gilbert, always conscientious about his contractual obligations, had an outline draft of the new opera ready by the end of 1882. Sullivan had a slight disagreement with the author about its merits when he first read it, but Gilbert obligingly made some changes and eventually Sullivan liked it enough to buckle down to work on the music.

In spite of the fact that the lyrics and music for *Princess Ida* were of higher caliber than its libretto—Martyn Green, one of the greatest Savoyards, thought that it "contains the very best of both Gilbert's and Sullivan's work"—it has never achieved the success, nor its songs the familiarity, of the other operas. It ran for only ten months, not up to the records of most Savoy productions. Perhaps Gilbert's parody of educated women was by 1884 neither current nor very funny, when degrees were being granted routinely at women's colleges in Oxford and Cambridge universities. (It's true there were still

Prince Hilarion, Cyril, and Florian plan their campaign to win Princess Ida. "We'll storm their bowers/With scented showers . . ."

". . . everybody says I'm such a disagreeable man!/And I can't think why!" King Gama broods.

The three young men, disguised as well-born maidens, ask Princess Ida if they may join her university.

some rather odd and special rules, such as that male visitors to a woman's rooms must keep both feet on the ground at all times while seated!) And Princess Ida's admonition to her women to "bind up [her brothers'] wounds—but look the other way" was certainly out of tune with the times that had already produced a Florence Nightingale!

The opera continued in the repertoire until, during World War II, its expensive scenery and costumes were victims of a bombing, and they have never been replaced. An ironic end to a production that made fun of women's inability to wage war boldly.

The opera's blank verse was difficult for some of the actors unaccustomed to its cadences, and Gilbert, the perfectionist, drilled them unmercifully. One actor, in desperation, said, "Look here, Sir! I will *not* be bullied! I know my lines!" "That may be, but you don't know mine!" Gilbert barked.

The part of the ugly, twisted King Gama, a contentious curmudgeon, was given to George Grossmith, who had the fun of parodying W. S. Gilbert, his taskmaster. The author was no less deadly when he turned his satirical pen to self-portraiture:

> *To compliments inflated I've a withering reply;*
> *And vanity I always do my best to mortify . . .*
>
> *To everybody's prejudice I know a thing or two;*
> *I can tell a woman's age in half a minute—and I do.*
> *But although I try to make myself as pleasant as I can,*
> *Yet everybody says I am a disagreeable man!*
> *And I can't think why!*

Meanwhile, Gilbert's collaborator was basking in honors and recognition. In May, 1883, at the age of forty-one, Dr. Sullivan became Sir Arthur Sullivan. As a knight, more would be expected of him, and *Princess Ida* was the first opera to be signed with his new title.

As usual, the weeks before the opening saw Sullivan working day and night to finish the music and the rehearsals. On January 4 he was in dreadful pain from "acute muscular rheumatism of head & neck." The next day's diary entry shows a man of iron will: "Resolved to conduct first performance of new opera at night but from state I was in it seemed hopeless. At 7 p.m. had another strong hyperdermic [sic] injection to ease the pain & a strong cup of black coffee to keep me awake—managed to get up & dressed & drove to the theatre more dead than alive . . . Tremendous house—usual reception. After the performance I turned faint & could not stand—was brought home by . . . Carte etc. & put to bed in dreadful pain."

Of the composer's heroic performance, *The Observer* wrote: "The success of the opera was never for a moment in doubt last night, and Sir Arthur Sullivan's music, while more ambitious in many of its elements than in his other comic operas, seems sure of gaining speedy popularity . . ."

Some three weeks later Sullivan wrote, "Told Carte of my resolve not to write any more 'Savoy' pieces."

"*If Gama fail . . . to bring the Princess Ida here . . .*
There's war between King Gama and ourselves!"

PRINCESS IDA

OR CASTLE ADAMANT

ACT I: *Pavilion in King Hildebrand's palace.*

GATHERED ON THE PARAPETS AND BATTLEMENTS of King Hildebrand's castle, the courtiers as well as the king's son, Hilarion, with his two companions, Cyril and Florian, impatiently scan the horizon through opera glasses, binoculars, and telescopes for the approach of King Gama. Gama's daughter, Princess Ida, was betrothed to two-year-old Hilarion when she was a year-old babe, and now twenty years have passed and this day will either bring rejoicing for the wedding or war between Gama and Hildebrand, depending on whether Ida has come with her father or not.

Hilarion wonders about the impending meeting with his "baby bride" and what changes the twenty years might have wrought. He was twice her age when they met—an inauspicious age difference, folk had said, for a happy marriage! But now:

> *Though she's twenty-one, it's true,*
> *I am barely twenty-two—*
> *False and foolish prophets you,*
> > *Twenty years ago!*

Hilarion tells his father he has heard that Princess Ida has shut herself away from the world with a band of women and "devotes herself to stern philosophies!" Hildebrand believes that "the loss of such a wife/Is one to which a reasonable man/Would easily be reconciled," but his son is not a reasonable man, and remembers their infant meeting fondly.

"Sons of Gama, hail! oh, hail!" Hildebrand's courtiers chorus, introducing one of the most comical entrances in all Gilbert and Sullivan. The trio of warriors clump on stage in heavy silver-gilt armor from helmet to toe, moving ponderously to the slow strains of music that tips its hat to Handel:

Dramatis Personae:

KING HILDEBRAND (Bass-baritone)

HILARION, His Son (Tenor)

CYRIL (Tenor)

FLORIAN (Baritone) — Hilarion's Friends

KING GAMA (Baritone)

ARAC (Bass-baritone)

GURON (Baritone) — His Sons

SCYNTHIUS (Bass-baritone)

PRINCESS IDA, Gama's Daughter (Soprano)

LADY BLANCHE, Professor of Abstract Science (Contralto)

LADY PSYCHE, Professor of Humanities (Soprano)

MELISSA, Lady Blanche's Daughter (Mezzo-soprano)

SACHARISSA (Soprano)

CHLOE (Soprano)   Girl Graduates

ADA

Soldiers, Courtiers, "Girl Graduates," "Daughters of the Plough," etc.

First produced at the Savoy Theatre on January 5, 1884.

"Gently, gently,/Evidently/We are safe so far,/After scaling/Fence and paling,/Here, at last, we are!"

There is an amusing story that Gilbert tells about *Princess Ida*'s opening night. Probably because of Sullivan's precarious state, Gilbert broke a precedent and forced himself to stay in the green room, pretending to read a newspaper. He relates: ". . . this gentleman, who had come over from Paris to enjoy the effect of his armour [it was supplied by the French firm of Le Grange et Cie], broke in upon me in a state of wild delight: *'Mais savez vous, Monsieur, que vous avez là un succès solide?'* I replied that the piece seemed to be going quite well. *'Mais vous êtes si calme,'* he exclaimed with a look of unbounded astonishment. I suppose he expected to see me kissing all the carpenters!''

"From the distant panorama
Come the sons of royal Gama. . . .
Sons of Gama, hail! oh, hail!"

Though the three fiercely bearded sons—one bright ginger, one blond, and one jet black—are a hard act to follow, King Gama introduces himself in a stingingly acid self-portrait. (Gilbert told George Grossmith, who played the part, "I meant it for myself: I thought it my duty to live up to my reputation.") Gama then proceeds to insult everyone and everything in King Hildebrand's court, getting as good as he gives from his hosts. Finally in exasperation Hildebrand exclaims, "Stop that tongue,/Or you shall lose the monkey head that holds it!" "Bravo!" yells Gama; "your King deprives me of my head,/That he and I may meet on equal terms!"

Gama then tells how Ida has turned Castle Adamant, one of his country houses, into a woman's university where she rules over a hundred girls. There are no males of any species within the walls—"excepting letter mails" (the trucks), driven by women. Not even a rooster—crowing is done by "an accomplished hen."

Hildebrand throws Gama and his sons into his dungeon as hostages while Hilarion, Cyril, and Florian determine to mount their own kind of assault against Castle Adamant:

Expressive glances
Shall be our lances,
    *And pops of Sillery**
    Our light artillery.

* A champagne popular at the time.

This tenderly musical trio spelling out the age-old male weapons of wooing—glances, champagne, flowers, love songs—is followed by Gama's sons' singing of a stridently martial air on their way to prison:

Who [are] longing for the rattle
Of a complicated battle—
For the rum-tum-tum
Of the military drum
    And the guns that go boom! boom!

ACT II: *Gardens of Castle Adamant.*

IN THE GARDENS OF CASTLE ADAMANT the girl graduates are seated
at the feet of Lady Psyche, who is lecturing on the evils of Man:

> *Man will swear and Man will storm—*
> *Man is not at all good form . . .*
>
> *Man's a ribald—Man's a rake,*
> *Man is Nature's sole mistake!*

Lady Blanche metes out punishments ordered by Princess Ida. One
girl is expelled for bringing men within the walls—"a set of chess-
men"—and one will lose three terms for sketching a perambulator in
her drawing book. "*Double* perambulator, shameless girl!"

Princess Ida enters to a chorus that hails her as a "mighty
maiden with a mission" and a "paragon of common sense." Wom-
en's mission, set forth in an aria that would not be out of place in
grand opera, is to wrest control of the world from men.

When Ida and her pupils leave, Lady Blanche, Professor of
Abstract Science, is alone, brooding on wresting control of the college from Ida, since she hates being second best. There is rivalry even
in this model female society where women are free and equal; nor is
it, in spite of its walls, free from troublemaking intruders.

For Hilarion and his friends have climbed over the college
walls—an experience that in itself has taught them some
useful knowledge. They've learned that when
they fall, it's apt to be on prickly

> *"Towards the empyrean heights*
> *Of every kind of lore,*
> *We've taken several easy flights,*
> *And mean to take some more."*

cactus, and that they don't like broken bottles atop a wall, that "spring-guns breathe defiance!" and finally that "burglary's a science! After all!" Still, Florian thinks a Woman's college is folly: "I'll teach them twice as much in half-an-hour outside it." And Cyril wonders if the object of the walls is not so much to keep men out as the maidens in.

By great good luck three of the girls have left the academic robes and caps they were mending, and the young men quickly don these for an instant disguise. None too soon, for here comes Princess Ida, deep in a book. The three new students start to bow, then catch themselves and curtsy demurely. At their request, the Princess graciously consents to accept them as students after extracting their promise never to marry any man. "Indeed we never will!" they vow piously.

After the Princess leaves, the three men laugh hilariously at their now being maids, whether they like it or not. But when Lady Psyche comes along and wonders at their unladylike mirth they quickly assume a more maidenly demeanor. Still, the jig is up. She is the sister of Florian and when she recognizes him, the others reveal their identities. She is especially glad to see Cyril, who was one of her earliest playfellows.

But she explains why all of the girls have promised to renounce mankind: "Man, sprung from an Ape, is Ape at heart." Darwin had written his theory of evolution only thirteen years earlier, and it would have been surprising if Gilbert *hadn't* risen to such delectable bait. Psyche's song about the Ape who loved a Lady is a two-edged blade. It could also be true of women who tried to be like men. The Ape shaves, docks his tail, buys white ties and dress suits, grows mustachios, joins a club—but it will not do:

While the Ape, despite his razor keen,
Was the apiest Ape that ever was seen! . . .

[And] *a Darwinian Man, though well-behaved,*
At best is only a monkey shaved!

While all of this has been going on, Melissa, Lady Blanche's young daughter, has entered and observed. She is enchanted by these strange new creatures, never having seen a man before, and is happy to be sworn to secrecy to protect them. She is about to leave with them and Lady Psyche but is called back by her mother. Lady Blanche suspects that the three new students she just glimpsed from afar are really men in disguise. "Two are tenors, one is a baritone!" she says. But when Melissa explains who they are and that Hilarion, who was plighted as a child to Princess Ida, has come to claim his bride, Lady Blanche sees a way to gain control of the school.

They are all called to a jolly al fresco lunch served by (homely) "Daughters of the Plough"—the ladies do not serve themselves!

"Would you know the kind of maid
Sets my heart aflame-a?
Eyes must be downcast and staid,
Cheeks must flush for shame-a!"

*"Some years ago
No doubt you know...
You gave your troth
Upon your oath
To Hilarion my son."*

*Merrily ring the luncheon bell!
Here in meadow of asphodel,
Feast we body and mind as well,
So merrily ring the luncheon bell!*

A good deal of wine is drunk, especially by Cyril, who sings an indiscreet and unmaidenly wooing song, grabs Lady Blanche at the "kiss me, kiss me," line and sends her screaming. Princess Ida realizes with horror that there are men among them and, in trying to flee, she falls into the stream. Brave Prince Hilarion leaps into the water after her and saves her, but the Princess orders the "coarse intruding spies" thrown into the dungeon and refuses to listen to her women's pleas for mercy. "I know not mercy, men in women's clothes!" she storms.

As the three hapless gentlemen are bound and marched off, Melissa comes running with the breathless announcement that "an armed band" of Hildebrand's men has battered down the castle gate. The troops rush in, with Gama's armor-clad sons (Princess Ida's very own brothers) among them, but handcuffed.

King Hildebrand takes a tough line with the Princess, pointing out that she made a vow to marry his son Hilarion:

*And I'm a peppery kind of King,
Who's indisposed to parleying
To fit the wit of a bit of a chit,
And that's the long and the short of it!*

Her brothers tell her the king will surely kill them and destroy her castle unless she marries Hilarion, and Hildebrand magnanimously offers a delay:

*We give you till to-morrow afternoon;
Release Hilarion, then, and be his bride,
Or you'll incur the guilt of fratricide!*

After this rousing, action-packed finale, the act ends picturesquely with the Princess surrounded by kneeling girls, King Hildebrand and his soldiers standing on rocks at the back and sides of the stage, and Ida, though but a girl, hurling defiance while all the others try to sway her as they sing:

*Hilarion's fair, and strong, and tall—
A worse misfortune might befall—
It's not so dreadful, after all,
To be his wife!*

ACT III: *Courtyard of Castle Adamant.*

ALONG THE OUTER WALLS AND COURTYARD of Castle Adamant the ladies, armed with battle-axes, are making military preparations. They are trying halfheartedly to be bellicose but they are really

*"So fail my cherished plans—so fails my faith—
And with it . . . all that comes of hope!"*

frightened silly, and between their heroic ''Death to the invader!/Strike a deadly blow'' and Melissa's ''Soldiers disconcert us. . . . Frightened maids are we!'' there is no doubt which is the honest sentiment.

Their princess enters with Lady Blanche and Lady Psyche and exhorts them all to prove that women educated to the task can meet man ''on his own ground'' and beat him. Her ''lady surgeon'' is

"...'twould be an error
To confess our terror,
So, in Ida's name,
Boldly we exclaim:
Death to the invader!"

alarmed at the prospect of healing the wounded. "And cut off real live legs and arms? . . . I wouldn't do it for a thousand pounds!" She would cut them off in theory, she explains, "again/With pleasure, and as often as you like,/But not in practice." Princess Ida angrily says she'll do it herself.

Then she sees her fusiliers armed with, of all things, axes! "Gilded toys!" Their rifles were left in the armory lest in the heat of battle they go off. "Go off yourselves!" orders the exasperated Princess. "*I* will discharge your rifles!" Nor is there gunpowder or explosive with which to blow the "bearded rascals" to shreds. Psyche, the director of the laboratory, suggests eyes flashing with rage and blistering tongues that will blow them up, rather than arts that brutalize the ladies' anger.

Ida finally sends all her useless women away and vows to meet the men alone. But she has been badly let down, and expresses her disappointment in the aria "I Built Upon a Rock."

In the midst of her despondency she is told that her father, King Gama, and her brothers request an audience. The King has suffered torments worse than death at Hildebrand's hands: he has been treated so well that he has nothing to complain about, and to a man of Gama's (read: Gilbert's) temperament that is the most exquisite torture:

> *Whene'er I spoke*
> *Sarcastic joke*
> *Replete with malice spiteful,*
> *This people mild*
> *Politely smiled,*
> *And voted me delightful!*

The Princess cannot bear her father's suffering, so she finally agrees to Hildebrand's request that a combat between Hilarion, Cyril, and Florian on one side and Arac, Guron, and Scynthius on the other decide the issue of her hand in marriage.

Hilarion and his friends are still wearing the women's scholastic gowns and are mercilessly twitted by King Gama. The three brothers do a funny song in which, on the verge of battle, they decide to divest themselves of their armor, piece by piece:

> *This helmet, I suppose,*
> *Was meant to ward off blows,*
> *It's very hot,*
> *And weighs a lot,*
> *As many a guardsman knows,*
> *So off that helmet goes.*

The same happens to cuirass, brassets, leg pieces ("I quite forget their name"—it is "jamb," if anyone is interested), and the brothers go into combat in tight-fitting undersuits rather like Superman's.

"Away, away—I'll meet these men alone
Since all my women have deserted me!"

"Consider this, my love," says Gama, "if your mamma Had looked on matters from your point of view . . . why where would you have been?"

And now we know why the armor had to be authentic, beautifully made pieces. Quite a good bit was made of it.

Princess Ida's brothers are beaten.

Ladies, my brothers all lie bleeding there!
Bind up their wounds—but look the other way.

The Princess has to resign her post and yield to Hilarion in marriage. She regrets that Posterity now will not bow in gratitude "at my exalted name." But Hildebrand points out that if all women were enlisted in her cause there would be no Posterity.

Before that logic there is no other recourse. Princess Ida says, "Take me, Hilarion," and then quotes directly from Tennyson's poem:

"We will walk the world
Yoked in all exercise of noble end!
And so through those dark gates across the wild
That no man knows! Indeed, I love thee—Come!"

Gilbert would of course have the last word.

As a finale, the Princess and Hilarion reprise his first-act trio with Cyril and Florian, the slow, lilting waltz "Expressive Glances," with the chorus intoning:

It were profanity
For poor humanity
To treat as vanity
   The sway of Love.
In no locality
Or principality
Is our mortality
   Its sway above!

THE MIKADO

OR THE TOWN OF TITIPU

ere's a how-de-do! . . . Here's a pretty mess! . . . Here's a pretty state of things!'' When Gilbert penned those lyrics some time in the last half of the year 1884, he may well have been describing the disastrous state of his and Sullivan's working relationship just a few months earlier. After a brilliantly successful collaboration on seven comic operas that had enriched both men and their producer, D'Oyly Carte, as well as the English musical stage, Gilbert and Sullivan were threatening to call it quits.

Perhaps Sullivan was stung by the critic of the *Musical Review*, who had written shortly after the composer was knighted, ''Some things that Mr. Arthur Sullivan may do, Sir Arthur ought not to do,'' and urged him to ''return to the sphere from which he has too long descended.'' In any event, Sullivan put Carte on notice, in response to the impresario's request for a new opera in six months, that it was impossible for him to do another such piece as he and Gilbert had been writing.

Gilbert, naturally, was appalled, at a loss to account for Sullivan's decision, and he reminded his collaborator ominously that they were bound by contract to supply Carte with an opera or they would be liable for any resulting losses. He just happened to have a possible libretto—it was a new treatment of his old favorite plot involving a magic lozenge that would turn the person who swallowed it into what he had always pretended to be. Sullivan had not liked the idea when it was first proposed. He did not like it any better now. Gilbert then wrote to him, ''with great reluctance,'' that he couldn't consent to construct a new plot.

Not the least of the author's problems might have been that he had exhausted the rich lode of ideas in *The Bab Ballads* that he had mined for earlier operas. For *Princess Ida* he had been forced to rehash a previously written play. Now, in middle age, he might have felt unable to invent a totally new situation, especially a plot such as

The Japanese Exhibition in London inspired the exotic sets and costumes for The Mikado, *though the plot was a typical Gilbertian romp through topsy-turvy land.*

Sullivan wanted—"in which no supernatural element occurs." But for both men there was too much at stake to discontinue their collaboration, and Gilbert eventually agreed to work on a plot that was not supernatural or improbable, to Sullivan's "inexpressible relief."

At which point the supernatural, if you will, took over anyhow and gave Gilbert his inspiration for the greatest of all their operas. He was pacing the floor in his sumptuously decorated study, worrying the plot problem, when there was a loud crash. His heavy tread had jarred loose an enormous Japanese executioner's sword hanging on the wall.

That sword later became a stage prop in the opera that it had inspired. For when Gilbert picked up the sword and held it in his hand, it "suggested the broad idea" of *The Mikado.* He did not have far to go for additional inspiration. In the nearby Knightsbridge section of London, the Great Japan Exhibition had recently opened, complete with a Japanese village whose oriental men and women dressed in their elegant robes were an exotic sight on the neighborhood streets near Albert Gate.

Evidently the Japanese idea found favor with Sullivan, for he gladly undertook to collaborate once more on an opera "without the supernatural or improbable elements."

The realm of probability, for Gilbert, had fairly far-flung borders. In a fanciful setting of medieval Japan, the Mikado and his Lord High Executioner (whose sword we have already met), a highborn noble called Pooh-Bah, a trio of charming schoolgirls, and a princeling disguised as a minstrel engage in a cheerful spoof of British manners, morals, and government. Of this G. K. Chesterton observed,

"I doubt if there is a single joke in the whole play that fits the Japanese. But all the jokes in the play fit the English."

Be that as it may, *The Mikado* has been performed in so many countries and in such varied styles that its material must have been more universal than even its originators could have dreamed. Its first run lasted for nearly two solid years in London, and it was also toured throughout Great Britain, Italy, Germany, Holland, and Scandinavia, played in the United States in over a hundred pirated as well as authorized (royalty-paying) productions, while among the foreign-language versions can be included Japanese, Chinese, and even Hindustani! Not to speak of, later, an all-black *Swing Mikado*; Mike Todd's *The Hot Mikado*, starring Bill Robinson; the *Black Mikado*; the *Cool Mikado*; and a jazz *Mikado* in Berlin, where Nanki-Poo Charlestoned in Oxford bags, Katisha wore tweeds, and Yum-Yum sang about not being shy while nude in a bathtub. It was probably the most lucrative stage property of its time.

Gratifying as the financial success of the opera must have been to the Savoy triumvirate, the "Captious Critic's" review in London's *The Illustrated Sporting and Dramatic News,* reflecting a nice blend of the paper's dual interests, must have pleased them with its appreciation of the smoothness of their joint efforts after a stormy interval:

One thing is very striking throughout the opera, and that is the fashion in which music and words are made to fit one another in both sound and sense. More than one of the songs was to me irresistibly suggestive of a coursing match with the two dogs, Words and Music, following the hare Idea neck and neck through all her twistings and windings.

The most popular of the Gilbert and Sullivan operas, The Mikado *has introduced the citizenry of Titipu to people all over the world. These are costume sketches for an early German production.*

THE MIKADO

OR THE TOWN OF TITIPU

ACT I: *Courtyard of Ko-Ko's official residence.*

THE COURTYARD OF KO-KO'S PALACE in the town of Titipu appears like a Japanese work of art, with its nobles standing and sitting in attitudes recognizable from the screens, fans, and the blue-and-white willowware so popular in the 1880s. The music for the chorus of nobles, ''We are gentlemen of Japan . . .'' also seems authentically Japanese, using the five-note scale of oriental music and its abrupt, rather jerky phrasing.

Gilbert took great pains always to set his scenes and dress his characters with the utmost authenticity. Then, on that sound foundation of reality, he took off into the blue of fun and nonsense and zany fantasy. So here we see the ''gentlemen of Japan'' splendidly attired in robes designed after Japanese authorities in pure Japanese fabrics. Gilbert found a male Japanese dancer and a geisha, or tea girl, at the Knightsbridge exhibition and hired them to teach the cast Japanese deportment: the peculiarly graceful pigeon-toed little shuffle with which women walked or ran in tiny, mincing steps; how to use a fan expressively, waving it, fluttering it, snapping it to indicate delight, coquetry, or anger; the typical giggling behind the fan; the sibilant hissing on an intake of breath that was conversational punctuation. The geisha did her coaching job remarkably well in spite of having only two words of English, ''Sixpence, please''—the price of the tea she sold at the Knightsbridge Japanese village teahouse. That being a perfect Gilbertian name, she was forever after ''Miss Sixpence Please'' and her mannerisms have been perpetuated in *Mikado* performances to this day.

The chorus of nobles, having established that we are indeed in Japan, are now joined by an excited young man carrying a Japanese guitar on his back and a bundle of ballads in his hand. He is Nanki-Poo and he is looking for the ''gentle maiden'' Yum-Yum, who is the ward of Ko-Ko. He delivers the first hit song of the opera, ''A

Dramatis Personae:

THE MIKADO OF JAPAN (Bass-baritone)

NANKI-POO, His Son, Disguised as a Wandering Minstrel, and in Love with Yum-Yum (Tenor)

KO-KO, Lord High Executioner of Titipu (Baritone)

POOH-BAH, Lord High Everything Else (Bass-baritone)

PISH-TUSH, a Noble Lord (Baritone)

GO-TO, a Noble Lord (Bass)

YUM-YUM (Soprano)
PITTI-SING (Mezzo-soprano) } Three Sisters— Wards of Ko-Ko
PEEP-BO (Soprano)

KATISHA, an Elderly Lady, in Love with Nanki-Poo (Contralto)

Chorus of School-Girls, Nobles, Guards, and Coolies

First produced at the Savoy Theatre on March 14, 1885.

Wandering Minstrel I,'' which gives us a hint of the young man's (and Sullivan's!) versatility. Starting out as a romantic ballad, his ''supple song'' shifts into a vigorous military march and then to a cheerfully rousing sea chanty.

A noble lord named Pish-Tush now asks what Nanki-Poo's business is with Yum-Yum and learns that the minstrel had seen the girl a year ago when he was a member of the town band. They fell in love,

''A wandering minstrel I—
A thing of shreds and patches . . .''

but Yum-Yum was betrothed to her guardian, Ko-Ko, "a cheap tailor," and Nanki-Poo saw that his suit was hopeless. Now, having heard that Ko-Ko was condemned to death for flirting, the minstrel has hurried back to try to claim Yum-Yum.

The nobleman Pish-Tush (his name was one of the few small gems remaining to be mined from *The Bab Ballads*—Pish-Tush-Pooh-Bah was a haughty character in "King Borria Bungalee Boo" and Gilbert got two names for *The Mikado* from it) tells of the Mikado's law

> *That all who flirted, leered or winked*
> *(Unless connubially linked),*
> *Should forthwith be beheaded.*

But the law was so distasteful that the town let Ko-Ko out on bail and made him Lord High Executioner, reasoning that since he was next to be decapitated, he couldn't chop off another's head without first cutting off his own. Nanki-Poo is amazed that Ko-Ko the tailor now holds the highest rank a citizen can attain, and of course remains engaged to Yum-Yum. The minstrel's cause seems lost.

There is worse to come, and it comes in the guise of Pooh-Bah, pompous, venal, and arrogant, who in true Darwinian fashion can trace his ancestry back to "a protoplasmal primordial atomic globule." He was born sneering, and he holds every major office of state concurrently, from First Lord of the Treasury to Archbishop of Titipu. His name, in lower case, has since been taken over into the English language for just such a person. His bad news is that Yum-Yum and Ko-Ko are to be married this very day:

> *And the brass will crash,*
> *And the trumpets bray,*
> *And they'll cut a dash*
> *On their wedding day.*
> *She'll toddle away, as all aver,*
> *With the Lord High Executioner!*

As Nanki-Poo wanders off in despair, the chorus of nobles calls out, "Defer, defer, / To the Lord High Executioner!" And Ko-Ko arrives, attended by the littlest boy available. The tiny attendant carries the Executioner's badge of office, a huge sword (on opening night Ko-Ko himself carried Gilbert's own double-handled sword). Ko-Ko assures the gentlemen that if ever he has to act in his professional capacity, there will be plenty of people whose loss would be society's gain. As a matter of fact, he's "got a little list . . . And they'll none of 'em be missed." The "little list" song has been updated frequently to keep the allusions topical, and it is always good for a few encores.

Ko-Ko discusses with Pooh-Bah, in his various official capacities, the possibility of financing his impending marriage out of public

"A Pooh-Bah paid for his services! I a salaried minion! But I do it! It revolts me, but I do it!"

money—and gets conflicting answers. It finally boils down to having to square "all these distinguished people," and Pooh-Bah says that "they wouldn't be sufficiently degraded in their own estimation unless they were insulted with a very considerable bribe." Ko-Ko promises to consider it, and adds that his bride is approaching and he would esteem any little compliment to her as a favor—"such as an abject grovel in a characteristic Japanese attitude." To which Rutland Barrington, the first Pooh-Bah, always added the exit line "No money—no grovel!" (and it has remained to this day).

Yum-Yum, as delicious as her name, appears with Peep-Bo and Pitti-Sing and the "train of little ladies," their schoolfellows, all attired in lovely Japanese silk kimonos from Liberty and Company. (In the 1880s it was a stunning surprise to discover that these were worn close to the body with no petticoats.) The three girls, fluttering their fans, and giggling, sing the showstopper:

Ko-Ko and Pooh-Bah in delicate negotiations over the price of "an abject grovel in a characteristic Japanese attitude."

> *Three little maids from school are we,*
> *Pert as a school-girl well can be,*
> *Filled to the brim with girlish glee,*
> *Three little maids from school!*

When Yum-Yum finally catches sight of Nanki-Poo and they are alone, she admits she does not love her guardian. "Modified rapture!" exclaims Nanki-Poo. He suggests she refuse to marry her guardian, and he will wait for her until she comes of age. But Yum-Yum isn't sure that "a wandering minstrel, who plays a wind instrument outside tea-houses" would be a suitable husband for the ward of the Lord High Executioner. Nanki-Poo wastes no time, takes no chances, in proving this practical young lady's love: he confesses that he is the Mikado's son, and immediately Yum-Yum respectfully Your-Highnesses him all over the place. Nanki-Poo explains that he has had to flee his father's court because, unluckily, he captivated the elderly, ugly, and strong-willed Lady Katisha and it was either marry her or die on the scaffold. If it wasn't for the law about flirting, he and Yum-Yum could . . . And Nanki-Poo shows her a number of delicious things they could do—"if it wasn't for the law":

> *So, in spite of all temptation,*
> *Such a theme I'll not discuss,*
> *And on no consideration*
> *Will I kiss you fondly thus—(Kissing her.)*
>
> *Let me make it clear to you,*
> *This is what I'll never do!*
> *This, oh, this, oh, this, oh, this—(Kissing her.)*

"Comes a train of little ladies
From scholastic trammels free,
Each a little bit afraid is,
Wondering what the world can be!"

As Nanki-Poo departs in one direction and Yum-Yum in another, Ko-Ko enters and gazes after his bride-to-be. "There she goes!" he says. "To think how entirely my future happiness is wrapped up in that little parcel!'' His future is also enclosed in a still smaller parcel, a letter from His Majesty the Mikado, delivered by the dignitaries Pooh-Bah and Pish-Tush. The Mikado threatens to abolish the post of Lord High Executioner and reduce Titipu to the rank of a village unless a beheading takes place within a month. This would be ruinous, but not one of the three wants to volunteer as victim, and Ko-Ko, in any case, could not successfully decapitate himself.

Ko-Ko, embracing Yum-Yum: ''At last, my bride that is to be!''

Their terrible dilemma is solved for them by Nanki-Poo, who arrives carrying a length of rope with which he plans to "terminate an unendurable existence." Ko-Ko prevails upon him not to spoil himself with a do-it-yourself job but to be beheaded handsomely by a professional. Nanki-Poo agrees only on condition that he can marry Yum-Yum and enjoy a month of wedded bliss with her first. Then, after the execution, Ko-Ko will be able to marry the widowed Yum-Yum. As Ko-Ko explains the arrangement to all the others, he adds:

Now I adore that girl with passion tender,
And could not yield her with a ready will,
Or her allot
If I did not
Adore myself with passion tenderer still!

There is great rejoicing at the saving of Titipu's status, and Pooh-Bah, noting that it would be an empty compliment to cry "Long life to Nanki-Poo!" since he has only a month to live, proposes that instead they toast him three times with a "Long life to you—till then!"

At the height of the jollity, ugly Katisha storms in, having tracked down the escaped object of her affections. In her imperative contralto she chastises Nanki-Poo and Yum-Yum and threatens to reveal the minstrel's true identity, but she is outshouted by a chorus of Japanese syllables: "O ni! bikkuri shakkuri to!"—among the many possible meanings of which is "So surprised, we hiccup! Bah!" It serves its purpose dramatically and contrapuntally, as Katisha rushes furiously to the rear of the courtyard, clearing the crowd away right and left. But the chorus prevails with a blithely melodic finale, fans aflutter like so many gorgeous butterflies.

ACT II: *Ko-Ko's garden.*

IN THE PICTURESQUE GARDEN OF KO-KO'S PALACE, Yum-Yum sits surrounded by maidens; they are preparing her bridal toilette. They sing one of Gilbert's loveliest lyrics:

Braid the raven hair—
Weave the supple tress—
Deck the maiden fair,
In her loveliness—
Paint the pretty face—
Dye the coral lip—
Emphasize the grace
Of her ladyship!
Art and nature, thus allied,
Go to make a pretty bride.

"Counting the House." In 1888, C. W. Allers made this backstage sketch of the Mikado *touring company in Hamburg.*

"Flutter, little heart, / Colour, come and go!
Modesty at marriage-tide / Well becomes a pretty bride!"

Pooh-Bah invites Ko-Ko: "Choose your fiction, and I'll endorse it!"

Nanki-Poo follows Ko-Ko's order to "Take Yum-Yum and marry Yum-Yum . . ."

Yum-Yum tells Peep-Bo and Pitti-Sing that she is the happiest girl in all Japan because today she will be marrying the man she loves best! But those two good friends soon have her in tears by reminding her how quickly her happiness will be cut short. When Nanki-Poo arrives, he finds his bride-to-be in tears. He cheers her by saying that when they're together they'll "call each second a minute—each minute an hour—each hour a day—and each day a year." That way they will have thirty years of married happiness to look forward to.

Ko-Ko joins them and tortures himself by witnessing their affectionate embraces, but he then addresses Yum-Yum as his "little bride that was to have been." She is delighted that it is not to be—until the awful truth outs: by the Mikado's law, the widow of a beheaded man must be buried alive! When Yum-Yum realizes what's in store for her, she turns to Nanki-Poo. "Darling—I don't want to appear selfish, and I love you with all my heart—I don't suppose I shall ever love anybody else half as much—but when I agreed to marry you—my own—I had no idea—pet—that I should have to be buried alive in a month!"

The difficulty is that if Nanki-Poo holds Yum-Yum to this marriage, she dies a hideous death, and if he releases her, she must marry Ko-Ko at once. It is this insuperable problem that prompts the song:

> *Here's a how-de-do!*
> *If I marry you,*
> *When your time has come to perish,*
> *Then the maiden whom you cherish*
> *Must be slaughtered, too!*
> *Here's a how-de-do!*

Never was a terrible predicament presented with greater hilarity—much comic business, with fans being snapped open and fluttered in dismay. The song has always drawn many encores and Martyn Green used to finish each encore with a flourish of a smaller and smaller fan produced from his kimono sleeve. His record was eight encores, and that final fan must have been minuscule.

The marriage is off, and Nanki-Poo determines to do away with himself that afternoon unless Ko-Ko will execute him at once. But, as it turns out, Ko-Ko can't kill anything—"Why, I never even killed a blue-bottle!" To make matters worse, the Mikado and his suite are fast approaching the town and will arrive in ten minutes. In desperation Ko-Ko arranges to draw up an affidavit of Nanki-Poo's execution, witnessed by all the officers of state who are embodied in Pooh-Bah, who will be happy to perjure themselves for a gross insult—cash on the barrelhead. The clinking bag of money clinches Pooh-Bah's signature(s).

In his terror, Ko-Ko is happy to give up Yum-Yum to Nanki-Poo. "Take Yum-Yum and marry Yum-Yum, only go away and never come back again."

It was a close call, for the strains of the "March of the Mikado's Troops" can now be heard approaching Ko-Ko's garden. This was a famous Japanese war march of the Imperial Japanese Army, the words (at one time erroneously believed to be "the foulest song ever sung in the lowest teahouse in Japan") and music of which were supplied to Sullivan as an authentic piece to herald the Mikado's entry.

He arrives, gorgeously attired, carried on a magnificent litter, with Katisha and other members of his court in attendance. He introduces himself grandly: "I'm the Emperor of Japan . . ." Katisha makes a strong point of being "his daughter-in-law elect" and is very likely the power behind the throne. In a famous song the Mikado lets it be known that he is humane, a true philanthropist:

> *My object all sublime*
> *I shall achieve in time—*
> *To let the punishment fit the crime—*
> *The punishment fit the crime;*
> *And make each prisoner pent*
> *Unwillingly represent*
> *A source of innocent merriment!*
> *Of innocent merriment!*

"From every kind of man
Obedience I expect;
I'm the Emperor of Japan—"

Then once again we have a brilliant patter song, as in the "little list," of the kind of persons we all know and hate, and what should be done to them by way of punishment. The Mikado laughs nastily between each verse, the audience hilariously all through the outrageous catalog of crimes and punishments.

When Ko-Ko presents his certificate of execution, the Mikado reads it and says, "My poor fellow, in your anxiety to carry out my wishes you have beheaded the heir to the throne of Japan!" The story is told that in one early performance, when George Grossmith was playing Ko-Ko, Gilbert came to him and said, "I am told, Mr. Grossmith, that in last night's performance when you were kneeling before the Mikado, he gave you a push and you rolled over completely on the floor." Grossmith started to explain that, in his interpretation—but was cut short with: "Whatever your interpretation, please omit that in future." Grossmith persisted: ". . . but I got a big laugh by it." "So would you if you sat on a pork pie."

Of all this the audiences were blissfully unaware. They laughed at the topsy-turvy world of the Mikado who goes to lunch to think over the punishment for Ko-Ko and Pooh-Bah and for Pitti-Sing for having falsely described how she soothed Nanki-Poo's last moments. The punishment should be "something humorous, but lingering, with either boiling oil or melted lead. Come, come, don't fret—I'm not a bit angry," insists the fierce-looking Emperor of Japan.

While the Mikado and Katisha are at lunch, Ko-Ko and Pooh-Bah find Nanki-Poo and beg him to present himself, alive, to his father, thereby absolving them of his death. But Nanki-Poo, though

"The threatened cloud has passed away,
And brightly shines the dawning day;
What though the night may come too soon,
We've years and years of afternoon!"

now married to Yum-Yum, is afraid of Katisha's wrath. Unless Ko-Ko will agree to marry the old hag himself, and so remove her amatory claims on him, he and Yum-Yum will leave on their honeymoon at once. With Katisha safely married, says Nanki-Poo, life will be "as welcome as the flowers in spring":

We welcome the hope that they bring,
Tra la,
Of a summer of roses and wine.

But Ko-Ko's version of the song is glummer:

The flowers that bloom in the spring,
Tra la,
Have nothing to do with the case.
I've got to take under my wing,
Tra la,
A most unattractive old thing,
Tra la,
With a caricature of a face . . .

Katisha, meanwhile, is mourning the death of Nanki-Poo, and when Ko-Ko comes a-wooing she is at first reluctant to have any traffic with her beloved's executioner. He woos and wins the formidable lady with a pack of flattering lies and a sad, lovelorn song, "Titwillow." But he really sweeps her off her feet and into an immediate marriage with:

Are you old enough to marry, do you think?
Won't you wait till you are eighty in the shade?
There's a fascination frantic
In a ruin that's romantic;
Do you think you are sufficiently decayed?

Katisha is momentarily furious when Nanki-Poo turns up alive and married, but relents and adds her powerful pleas to the Mikado for everyone to be pardoned. That august Emperor of Japan is a bit bewildered by it all, especially by Ko-Ko's complicated explanation, but he pardons everyone in sight and pronounces that "Nothing could possibly be more satisfactory!"

RUDDIGORE

OR THE WITCH'S CURSE

The Victorian stage in the mid-nineteenth century thrived on the most lurid melodramas peopled by hammy stock characters: the wicked, mustache-twirling baronet; the virtuous maiden; the country swain; a mad or half-mad character. What could be more amusing than, from the sophisticated vantage point of the late 1880s, to parody one of these extravagant plots and its hackneyed roles? One had only to exaggerate the overblown silliness of a ''meller-drammer'' a little and the line would be crossed into hilarious caricature.

That was precisely what Gilbert proposed to Sullivan early in 1886, although *The Mikado* was still spinning gold and there was no pressure to get a new opera on the boards. Gilbert would need only to revamp his *Ages Ago*, the play that, by coincidence, was the one in rehearsal that day in 1868 at the Royal Gallery of Illustration when he and Arthur Sullivan first met. To have a plot ready to hand was certainly a strong incentive for Gilbert, that avid borrower of his own material. Sullivan was less enthusiastic about the subject, but he preferred it to another ''magic lozenge'' plot that Gilbert had suggested a few months before. So he agreed to write the music—but not until he had attended to other, more pressing business.

He was committed to composing an oratorio based on Henry Wadsworth Longfellow's *The Golden Legend* for the October Leeds Festival; he had reluctantly promised the Prince of Wales he would set an ode of Tennyson's to music for the Colonial and Indian Exhibition; Franz Liszt was visiting London, and it fell to England's most illustrious composer to escort the venerable Hungarian musician around town. And there was his own pursuit of happiness—race meetings, garden parties, concerts, theater, yachting, often in the company of the dazzling Mrs. Ronalds (referred to in Sullivan's diary as LW for Little Woman). To that same diary Sullivan complained, ''How am I to get through this year's work? Do they think me a barrel-organ? They turn a handle and I disgorge music of any mood to order.''

Robin: ''I know a youth who loves
          a little maid—
          (Hey, but his face is a sight
          for to see!)''
Rose: ''I know a maid who loves a
          gallant youth,
          (Hey, but she sickens as the
          days go by!)''

Sir Despard Murgatroyd, of Ruddigore, the archetype of baronial villainy in old melodramas.

After his successful presentation of his oratorio at Leeds, *The World* fervently applauded "the Mozart of England." And Gilbert's note of hearty congratulations closed with the information that the libretto was finished, subject to any alterations that Sullivan might want to suggest. The urgency to buckle down to it is unmistakable in spite of the velvet glove that held the pen: "I don't expect you will want to turn to our work at once without any immediate rest, but if you do, I can come up any day and go through the MS with you."

Despard tells Mad Margaret:
"I once disliked you; now
that I've reformed,
How I adore you!"

Ruddygore was scheduled to be presented in three months. Sullivan, as usual, came down to the wire, writing and scoring day and night. Not until a week before the opening did he complete the music. Though the cast was, as always, well rehearsed by the martinet Gilbert, opening night was not without its problems. In the second act, when the Murgatroyd ancestral portraits come to life and descend from their frames, the frames refused to open on time; the second encore for Dick Dauntless's hornpipe was spoiled by the orchestra's slow tempo, "whereat Sir Arthur was obviously—and audibly—irate"; but worst of all, in spite of general enthusiasm and even some cheering, there were shouts and cries from the gallery of "Take off this rot! Give us back *The Mikado*!" The critic of the *Pall Mall Budget* put his finger neatly on the predicament: "It is the misfortune of Messrs Gilbert and Sullivan that they are their own rivals, and every new work makes their task harder."

The severest criticism was leveled at the title, which included the shockingly vulgar "ruddy" (a euphemism for the unspeakable "bloody"); it might be all right to say in a men's club, but not by ladies, "on whose lips such a title would scarcely sound pretty!" Gilbert had intended "ruddy gore" to mean, in all innocence, melodramatic red blood. Still, he bowed to the dissenting voices and changed the spelling to *Ruddigore* less than ten days into the run. In New York, where the opera opened in February, 1887, it remained *Ruddygore*—Americans, though prudish about many things, having no sensitivity about that word.

The opera had a run of 288 performances, or more than a year, at the Savoy, and when George Edwardes, a London stage manager, called it a failure, Gilbert was quick to point out that it had lined his pockets with a good £7,000, and: "I could do with a few more such failures."

Ruddigore languished, after its original run, for thirty years, when Rupert D'Oyly Carte revived it. Then, in the 1920s, parodies of musical melodrama had quite a vogue and *Ruddigore* remained in the repertoire. In 1937 the *Manchester Guardian*'s critic wrote: "It is incomprehensible that *Ruddigore* should ever have been considered less attractive than the other comic operas in the Savoy series." To Gilbert's ears that would have been sweeter music than any tune of Sullivan's.

W. Russell Flint's illustrations portray Dick Dauntless meeting Rose Maybud, and Mad Margaret in the "picturesque tatters" designed for her by Gilbert.

RUDDIGORE

OR THE WITCH'S CURSE

ACT I: *The fishing village of Rederring, in Cornwall.*

IN REDERRING, A CORNISH FISHING VILLAGE, Rose Maybud's cottage is besieged by a chorus of "professional bridesmaids." Rose, the village beauty, is the last eligible maiden, and the girls, who are the only such group in the world, are concerned because their services haven't been needed for six long months. If there isn't a wedding soon to demand their talents, they fear they will be "disendowed." And so they sing to the closed door:

> *Rose, all glowing*
> > *With virgin blushes, say—*
> *Is anybody going*
> > *To marry you to-day?*

Dame Hannah, Rose's aunt, comes out to tell the girls that they are beseeching in vain; Rose is not interested in any of her suitors. The desperate bridesmaids then ask Hannah—"you're a nice old person"—if she won't oblige them by marrying someone. She explains that she is pledged to "an eternal maidenhood," having once been betrothed to a godlike youth who turned out to be one of the bad baronets of Ruddigore, Sir Roderic Murgatroyd. Madly as she loved him, she left him then and there, and he has since died.

"All baronets are bad," says one of the bridesmaids; "was he worse than other baronets?" It was indeed a convention of the melodramas of the time for the villain to be a baronet, but Sir Roderic and his family were specially accursed, each baronet being forced by a witch's hex to commit one crime a day forever, or die. Eventually, over the generations, conscience gets the upper hand, the baronet vows to sin no more—and he dies, leaving his heir to fulfill the terms of the curse.

Now Rose Maybud, the pure heroine caricatured, comes out of the cottage carrying a basket full of goodies for deserving villagers.

Dramatis Personae:

SIR RUTHVEN MURGATROYD, Disguised as Robin Oakapple, a Young Farmer (Baritone)

RICHARD DAUNTLESS, His Foster-Brother—a Man-o'-war's-man (Tenor)

SIR DESPARD MURGATROYD, of Ruddigore, a Wicked Baronet (Baritone)

OLD ADAM GOODHEART, Robin's Faithful Servant (Bass)

ROSE MAYBUD, a Village Maiden (Soprano)

MAD MARGARET (Mezzo-soprano)

DAME HANNAH, Rose's Aunt (Contralto)

ZORAH (Soprano) ⎫
⎬ Professional Bridesmaids
RUTH (Mezzo-soprano) ⎭

Ghosts:

SIR RUPERT MURGATROYD, the First Baronet; SIR JASPER MURGATROYD, the Third Baronet; SIR LIONEL MURGATROYD, the Sixth Baronet; SIR CONRAD MURGATROYD, the Twelfth Baronet; SIR DESMOND MURGATROYD, the Sixteenth Baronet; SIR GILBERT MURGATROYD, the Eighteenth Baronet; SIR MERVIN MURGATROYD, the Twentieth Baronet;
and

SIR RODERICK MURGATROYD, the Twenty-first Baronet (Bass)

Chorus of Officers, Ancestors, Professional Bridesmaids, and Villagers

TIME: *Early in the nineteenth century.*

First produced at the Savoy Theatre on January 22, 1887.

"When the buds are blossoming . . . Lovers choose a wedding day—
Life is love in merry May!"

She also carries a book of etiquette that is her bible, and she tells her aunt that any man she could love would have to measure up to its precepts. Her aunt suggests Robin Oakapple, a young farmer, who "combines the manners of a Marquis with the morals of a Methodist." But Robin, who conveniently appears at this moment, is so shy he cannot speak to her except about the weather, and etiquette forbids her to do more than follow his lead. Robin awkwardly asks to consult Rose "about a friend," and here ensues one of Sullivan's loveliest ballads, "I Know a Youth Who Loves a Little Maid."

When the young couple have finished their duet, Rose goes about her good deeds. As Robin looks after her longingly, he is joined by Old Adam, who addresses him as Sir Ruthven (pronounced *Rivven*) Murgatroyd. The truth outs—twenty years ago Ruthven fled to this village rather than succeed to the baronetcy and be forced to commit a crime a day. His younger brother, Despard, believing him dead, has succeeded to the accursed title. Adam now tells him that his foster brother, Richard Dauntless, has returned from sea and is in the village.

The bridesmaids flock around the victorious mariner, who spins them a salty yarn about his exploits:

The Professional Bridesmaids of Rederring hope that somebody "will marry Rose today."

> *I shipped, d'ye see, in a Revenue sloop,*
>   *And, off Cape Finistere,*
>   *A merchantman we see,*
>   *A Frenchman, going free,*
>   *So we made for the bold Mounseer,*
>   *D'ye see?*
> *We made for the bold Mounseer.*

Richard winds up his tale of the encounter with the French frigate, from which his sloop fled—"We had pity on a poor Parley-voo!"—with a spirited hornpipe.

The foster brothers greet each other warmly and Robin confesses his love for Rose: ". . . happy the girl who gets me, say I. But I'm timid . . . shy—nervous—modest—retiring—diffident—and I cannot tell her." Richard volunteers to do Robin's wooing. His foster brother, who'd give his right arm for one-tenth of the sailor's assurance, admits that he is handicapped by "a diffident nature," although he knows what is needed for success:

> *If you wish in the world to advance,*
> *Your merits you're bound to enhance,*
>   *You must stir it and stump it,*
>   *And blow your own trumpet,*
> *Or, trust me, you haven't a chance!*

When Richard meets Rose, however, he is completely bowled over by her beauty, and in his "rough, common-sailor fashion" he tells her she's the lass for him. Rose accepts his suit.

When Robin and the bridesmaids appear, Robin thinks his

sailor-brother was victorious on his behalf, and he embraces Rose. Upon consideration, Rose disengages herself from Richard: "... he is but a lowly mariner, and very poor withal." She attaches herself to Robin: "... thou art a tiller of the land, and thou hast fat oxen ... a considerable dairy farm and much corn and oil!" Excusing her fickleness to Richard in nautical terms—"Hearts often tack"—she and Robin leave happily, while Richard goes off weeping, though determined to put up a fight for the girl.

An extraordinary creature now appears, dressed in picturesque tatters, barefoot, and with wisps of straw in her hair. Gilbert himself designed the original costume, and in Mad Margaret he has created a parody of Ophelia, even to the pathos of Margaret's

> No crime—
> 'Tis only
> That I'm
> Love-lonely!
> That's all!

She has been mad ever since Sir Despard, the current bad baronet of Ruddigore, trifled with her affections and left her.

Despard is planning to abduct Rose Maybud for today's crime and when Rose appears, Margaret asks, "You are Rose Maybud? ... Strange! They told me she was beautiful." Rose confides that she is to be married to someone this very day, and Margaret, no longer jealous, tells her to hide because Sir Despard and his evil crew of "Bucks and Blades" are coming to Rederring. "They are all mad—quite mad! ... They sing choruses in public," she adds by way of explanation. Mad Margaret and Rose tiptoe off.

The opera's bucks and blades, originally costumed by Gilbert in the authentic military dress uniforms of twenty regiments, today are the glass of Victorian male fashion, a sight to behold as they enter with the chorus of bridesmaids. To explain their being all dressed up in a tiny Cornish village, the men sing:

> When thoroughly tired
> Of being admired
> By ladies of gentle degree—degree,
> With flattery sated,
> High-flown and inflated,
> Away from the city we flee—we flee!

Every young man in the village is in love with Rose, who lives modestly with Dame Hannah, her aunt.

Hannah tells the fascinated bridesmaids the legend of the horrendous Murgatroyd curse.

Rose Maybud, discovering that Robin is the real wicked Baronet, tells the reformed Sir Despard: "Take me—I am thy bride!"

Sir Despard joins them and explains that he likes to get his crime over "the first thing in the morning," and then he can do good. "To-day I carry off Rose Maybud and atone with a cathedral!" He tells how he is at the mercy of his portrait gallery, where his ancestors "step down from their frames" and threaten him if he hasn't committed his daily crime. He mutters darkly about revenge: "I will give them all to the Nation, and nobody shall ever look upon their faces again!"

Richard Dauntless interrupts the baronet to reveal that his elder brother, Sir Ruthven, is living under the name of Robin Oakapple in this very village, where he plans to marry Rose Maybud today. Despard, in a cry from his unwillingly wicked heart, exclaims, "Free—free at last! Free to live a blameless life, and to die beloved and regretted by all who knew me!" And he disrupts the oncoming bridal party and claims Robin as Sir Ruthven Murgatroyd.

Poor Rose begs her bridegroom-to-be to deny this, but as he is still Robin, the "pure and blameless peasant," he cannot tell a lie. "When I'm a bad Bart. I will tell taradiddles!" he promises. But Rose will have none of the newly wicked baronet and turns instead to Sir Despard. "Take me—I am thy bride!" He, being a newly virtuous person, now says he must keep his vow to Mad Margaret. In desperation Rose turns to the foster brother:

> Richard, of him I love bereft,
>   Through thy design,
> Thou art the only one that's left,
>   So I am thine!

And they embrace. Robin storms off as the others are singing of happiness, and when he returns he has exchanged his farmer's straw hat for the bad baronet's silk topper. He flings a villainous black cape about his shoulders, seizes a hunting crop, and cracks his whip at poor Old Adam, who will now have to do his evil bidding.

ACT II: The picture gallery in Ruddigore Castle.

WE ARE IN RUDDIGORE CASTLE'S GREAT picture gallery, its walls hung with full-length portraits of all the baronets of Ruddigore from the time of James I.

The newest baronet and his man, Adam, enter and the change in them is shocking. Robin wears "the haggard aspect of a guilty roué"; his formerly benign and faithful old retainer is now a "wicked steward." Robin sings:

> I once was as meek as a new-born lamb,
>   I'm now Sir Murgatroyd—ha! ha!
>   With greater precision
>   (Without the elision),
>   Sir Ruthven Murgatroyd—ha! ha!

Dick Dauntless gives Sir Despard the welcome news that the curse and title belong to his elder brother Ruthven, and that he is free.

The problem is that he is conscientious about doing the right thing—in this case the wrong thing—and is finding it hard to think up a daily crime. Adam is not much help in inventing one for him.

When Dick Dauntless brings Rose Maybud and her company of bridesmaids to the castle for the baronet's permission to marry, Robin tries to sound menacing and talks darkly of dungeons. But Dick produces a Union Jack, which he waves above his fiancee: ''. . . while this glorious rag floats over Rose Maybud's head, the man does not live who would dare to lay unlicensed hand upon her!'' ''Foiled,'' snarls Robin, ''—and by a Union Jack!'' (This patriotic spoof went over well everywhere but in Ireland, where the Union Jack was anathema.) Rose appeals to Robin, in remembrance of their love, to give his consent to her marriage with Dick; moved by her entreaty, he agrees.

Alone in the gallery, Robin wonders if the petty crimes he has committed in his week as wicked baronet will be considered bad enough by his ancestors. He implores them to be merciful in judging him. The stage darkens, there is a fortissimo passage on the timpani (not only a dramatic device but a practical one as well, to cover any mechanical sounds of the frames opening), and when the lights come up again the ancestral portraits have sprung to life. They step from their frames, and sternly march, singing, round the stage. Finally Sir Roderic, the latest-deceased baronet, descends from his frame, with a terrible ''Beware! beware! beware!'' He and the others sing of the ghosts' jolly times:

> *When the night wind howls in the chimney cowls, and the bat*
> *in the moonlight flies,*
> *And inky clouds, like funeral shrouds, sail over the midnight*
> *skies—*
> *When the footpads quail at the night-bird's wail, and black*
> *dogs bay at the moon,*
> *Then is the spectres' holiday—then is the ghosts' high-noon!*
> *Ha! Ha!*
> *Then is the ghosts' high-noon!*

Robin is forced to list the crimes he has committed this first week, hoping for their approval. A false income-tax return (''Everybody does that''); he shot a fox—very bad form among hunting people (''That's better''); he forged a check of Adam's (Adam had no banker, so it doesn't count); he disinherited his only son (he has no son, so it doesn't count) . . . All in all a disappointing performance. Robin must commit a first-rate crime—like carrying off a lady—or he will die in agony, the ghosts of his ancestors insist. After a small sample of the agony, Robin agrees. The ghosts return to their frames, and once again are merely portraits.

Robin orders Old Adam to go to the village and carry off any maiden—''I don't care which''—but at once. Alone, he sings:

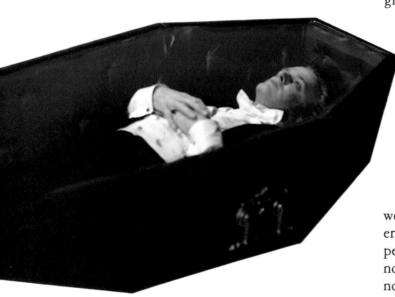

''Baronet of Ruddigore,
Last of our accursèd line,
Down upon the oaken floor—
Down upon those knees of thine.''

''How dreadful when an innocent heart
Becomes, perforce, a bad young Bart. . . .''

Henceforth all the crimes that I find in the Times,
   I've promised to perpetrate daily;
To-morrow I start, with a petrified heart,
   On a regular course of Old Bailey.

This song, of typical Gilbertian wit, was later dropped from performances, and is seldom heard today.

While Robin is trying to become even more wicked, Despard has grown painfully respectable. He and his wife Margaret are scarcely recognizable when they enter. Both are dressed in sober black as befits people who rule a National School where the poor are educated. When they execute one of their "blameless dances," cutting "respectable capers," we can believe Despard's "The duties are dull, but I'm not complaining." Margaret has occasional lapses from her proper primness into the old madness, but if Despard says firmly, "Basingstoke," she pulls herself together.

They have come to persuade Robin to defy his ancestors and give up the life of crime (the patter trio—with "So it really doesn't matter, matter, matter, matter, matter!"—is not only the clincher but a palpable hit), and he is ready to agree, when Adam returns with the day's crime accomplished. He has abducted a maiden—Dame Hannah! Robin listens to the old woman's outraged diatribe and mutters, "And this is what it is to embark upon a career of unlicensed pleasure!"

Hannah has a very small poniard and this she throws to Robin while taking a formidable longsword from one of the armed ancestors. She is now prepared to fight for her honor, fair and square. Her fierce and vigorous defense soon has her abductor backed into a corner, utterly cowed. In an agony of terror Robin calls out to a portrait, "Roderic! Uncle! Save me!"

Roderic steps out of his frame, but when he sees the old woman he cries, "Little Nannikin!" He then sends Robin away like a naughty schoolboy and he and his love, happily reunited, sing a meaningful ballad about a "pretty little flower" and a "great oak tree."

Their tender rendezvous is interrupted by Robin's unmannerly return with all of the cast and the bridesmaids following close upon his heels. He is very excited by an idea that has just struck him and he explains it to his uncle. According to the family curse, a baronet of Ruddigore must commit a crime each day or he will die. Therefore, his refusal to commit a daily crime is "tantamount to suicide. . . . But suicide is, itself, a crime." By that logic, Roderic "ought never to have died at all!" "I see," exclaims Roderic. "Then I'm practically alive!"

Now Robin turns to Rose, who had loved him passionately, madly, when he was a "simple farmer." If he should turn out not to be a "bad baronet" after all, she can love him—"Madly, passionately!"—once again. Dick Dauntless is not happy with this denoue-

"From grey tomb-stones are gathered the
         bones that once were women and men,
And away they go, with a mop
         and a mow, to the revel that
         ends too soon . . ."

ment, but finds a port in the storm when he is paired off with a pretty bridesmaid:

Like an honest British sailor, I reply,
  That with Zorah for my missis,
  There'll be bread and cheese and kisses,
Which is just the sort of ration I enjye!

Robin sings:

Having been a wicked baronet a week,
Once again a modest livelihood I seek,
  Agricultural employment
  Is to me a keen enjoyment,
For I'm naturally diffident and meek!

The final chorus, a reprise from the Act I finale, is more amusing for its business and dance steps than for its song. Old Adam comes out bearing a tray with a decanter of sherry and glasses already filled. There is some funny pantomime as Margaret refuses for Despard, who would have liked a nip, and herself; Dick Dauntless switches a half-filled glass from himself to Zorah, taking her full one. Robin and Rose toast each other as all sing the very apt words

For happy the lily
  That's kissed by the bee;
And, sipping tranquilly,
  Quite happy is he;
And happy the filly
  That neighs in her pride;
But happier than any,
A pound to a penny,
A lover is, when he
  Embraces his bride!

The merry bridesmaids peep from behind their bed curtains at the mass-marriage finale.

THE YEOMEN OF THE GUARD

OR THE MERRYMAN AND HIS MAID

Nearly a year passed between the lowering of the Savoy Theatre curtain on the 288th—and final—performance of *Ruddigore*'s run and its rising on the first night of a new production, *The Yeomen of the Guard*, on October 3, 1888. In the interim the Savoy presented revivals of *H.M.S. Pinafore, The Pirates of Penzance*, and *The Mikado*.

If the public was disappointed that there was no new Gilbert and Sullivan opera to mark Queen Victoria's Golden Jubilee in the last half of 1877, they were not altogether mollified by the first Savoy revival of the popular old work *Pinafore*. D'Oyly Carte, exerting subtle pressure on the composer to collaborate again with Gilbert, cabled Sullivan, who was on the Continent: "Present revival artistic success but no money. Do not believe any other revival will be much better. My chance of running present establishment seems to be to rush on new piece. If this impractical must try to let theatre."

Gilbert, meanwhile, was still trying to get his magic lozenge plot past Sullivan, but the composer's response was consistently negative. Then one lucky day Gilbert was waiting for a train at suburban Uxbridge Station. There across the platform was the Tower Furnishing Company's poster of a scarlet-uniformed "Beefeater" standing before the Tower of London. As Gilbert later told his biographers, Dark and Grey, this set him thinking. The glory years of Tudor England under Queen Elizabeth were not unlike the prosperous decades during the reign of Queen Victoria, on whose empire the sun never set. What could be more fitting than for one great age to salute another in an opera laid in sixteenth-century London at the historic Tower? Gilbert made haste to get an outline down on paper.

On Christmas day, Gilbert and Carte visited Sullivan with the story. "Gilbert read plot of new piece . . . immensely pleased with it," Sullivan jotted in his diary. "Pretty story, no topsy-turvydom, very human, and funny also." A descriptive billing was decided on then and there—"an entirely new and original opera"—to make

Wilfred Shadbolt, the Head Jailer and Assistant Tormentor, complains, "I didn't become a head jailer because I like head-jailing. I didn't become an assistant tormentor because I like assistant-tormenting."

"Tower warders,/Under orders,/Gallant pikemen, valiant sworders!/Brave in bearing,/Foemen scaring . . ."

clear that Gilbert and Sullivan in this presentation were not dealing with another lightweight *comic* opera.

The title itself underwent several changes from the obvious *The Tower of London* to *The Tower Warder*, then to *The Beefeater* ("a good, sturdy, solid name, conjuring up picturesque associations and clearly telling its own tale at once," wrote Gilbert at one point), and finally to *The Yeomen of the Guard,* or *The Merryman and His Maid.*

Buoyed by Sullivan's enthusiasm, and possibly enthralled himself by the romantic atmosphere and history of the Tower, Gilbert spent hours researching the place for local color and sketching the

To the tolling of the chapel bells, the Headsman takes his place at the block, his ax ready for Colonel Fairfax's execution.

Beefeaters. He even went so far as to read Shakespeare for the rhythms and locutions of Elizabethan English. "If you promise me faithfully not to mention this to a single person, not even to your dearest friend," he confessed to George Grossmith, who was to play Jack Point, the Merryman, "I don't think Shakespeare rollicking." Nevertheless, Gilbert managed to be rollicking and somewhat Shakespearean at the same time when his clown, Jack Point, sings:

> *It's the song of a merryman, moping mum,*
> *Whose soul was sad, and whose glance was glum,*
> *Who sipped no sup, and who craved no crumb,*
>   *As he sighed for the love of a ladye.*

Sullivan was able to start composing the music for *The Yeomen of the Guard* in July, 1888, working in the country, at Fleet in Hampshire. His music reflected the atmosphere of Tudor England that Gilbert had so carefully built into his libretto and, hearing the delicate melodies and elegant part-songs, no one could have guessed that while composing them Sullivan was wretched and "a very sick man." He himself confided to his diary about the opening night on October 3: "Tired and nervous. Crammed house . . . I was awfully nervous and continued so until the duet 'Heighday' which settled the fate of the Opera. Its success was tremendous . . . After that everything went on wheels, and I think its success is even greater than *The Mikado*. Nine Encores."

Gilbert, his opening-night nervousness exacerbated by a flare-up of painful gout and his uneasiness about the serious plot, hid out at the Drury Lane Theatre, where *The Armada* was playing. He returned to the Savoy in time to take his bows with Sullivan, and one must suppose that, at such moments of mutual triumph, all artistic differences between the two men evaporated in a golden glow.

The Lieutenant of the Tower questions Wilfred and Jack Point about Fairfax's disappearance: "Who fired that shot? At once the truth declare!"

THE YEOMAN OF THE GUARD

OR THE MERRYMAN AND HIS MAID

ACT I: *Tower Green.*

EVEN BEFORE THE CURTAIN RISES ON *The Yeomen of the Guard* the scene is set musically by one of Sullivan's more impressive symphonic overtures. The "Tower of London" motif rings out imperiously, interwoven with more tender melodies and poignant passages that will recur in the songs of the opera's colorful characters. Never has so-called "light opera" been served with such imposing musicianship; it is no wonder that Gilbert and Sullivan's spell over audiences has prevailed for over a hundred years.

When the curtain rises on Tower Green, the stage is empty save for one slight young woman at her spinning wheel. In place of a rousing chorus singing an amusing Gilbertian lyric, solitary Phoebe holds the stage, moping and sighing as she spins, and her plaintive love song, "When Maiden Loves, She Sits and Sighs," is, in Gilbert's words, "tearful in character." Hardly the upbeat beginning that Savoyards had come to expect, but it suited Sullivan's desire for a more truly operatic libretto from Gilbert with emphasis on what he called the "human element."

Phoebe's song finishes with a sad "Ah me!" and she is weeping when Wilfred Shadbolt, Head Jailer and Assistant Tormentor, appears. He is plainly in love with Phoebe and she, just as plainly, despises him for his brutal profession and for the fact that his prisoner, the admirable Colonel Fairfax, is to be executed that evening. She has no sympathy for the torturer—who is being tortured himself by pangs of jealousy.

The mood shifts when a crowd of men and women appear, followed by a company of Yeomen of the Guard, who march on bravely chanting:

> *Tower Warders,*
> *Under orders,*
> *Gallant pikemen, valiant sworders!*

Dramatis Personae:

SIR RICHARD CHOLMONDELEY, Lieutenant of the Tower (Bass-baritone)

COLONEL FAIRFAX, Under Sentence of Death (Tenor)

SERGEANT MERYLL, of the Yeomen of the Guard (Bass-baritone)

LEONARD MERYLL, His Son (Tenor)

JACK POINT, a Strolling Jester (Baritone)

WILFRED SHADBOLT, Head Jailer and Assistant Tormentor (Bass-baritone)

THE HEADSMAN

FIRST YEOMAN

SECOND YEOMAN

FIRST CITIZEN

SECOND CITIZEN

ELSIE MAYNARD, a Strolling Singer (Soprano)

PHOEBE MERYLL, Sergeant Meryll's Daughter (Mezzo-soprano)

DAME CARRUTHERS, Housekeeper to the Tower (Contralto)

KATE, Her Niece (Soprano)

Chorus of Yeomen of the Guard, Gentlemen, Citizens, etc.

TIME: *Sixteenth century.*

First produced at the Savoy Theatre on October 3, 1888.

Jack Point and Elsie attempt to amuse the Tower crowds with "The Merryman and His Maid."

The Yeomen are splendidly authentic in the scarlet "Beefeaters" uniforms of Tudor England, with H R (for King Henry VIII) blazoned across their chests. They and Dame Carruthers, the Tower's housekeeper, launch into a song that traces the Tower's history:

When our gallant Norman foes
  Made our merry land their own,
    And the Saxons from the Conqueror were flying,
At his bidding it arose,
  In its panoply of stone,
    A sentinel unliving and undying.

It is at once clear that in this opera Gilbert intends to instruct as well as to amuse.

When they all march off, Phoebe and her father, Sergeant Meryll, commiserate that no reprieve has come yet for Colonel Fairfax, who twice in the past has saved the Sergeant's life. Phoebe's brother, Leonard, is due to arrive soon, rewarded for bravery in action with an appointment to the Yeomen of the Guard. Father and daughter are hopeful that Leonard will bring the reprieve with him from the Court at Windsor, but when the brave young man appears, he is empty-handed. "I would I had brought better news," he tells them soberly. "I'd give my right hand—nay, my body—my life, to save his!"

At this, the Sergeant is inspired to devise an escape for Colonel Fairfax: Leonard is to stay hidden for a time and, since no one has yet seen the new appointee, the Colonel can be passed off as Leonard Meryll, dressed in a Yeoman's uniform and minus his beard. Phoebe will get the key to the condemned man's cell from her "sour-faced admirer," Wilfred Shadbolt. "I *think* . . . I can get anything I want from Wilfred," Phoebe says demurely; "you may leave that to me."

Fairfax is being marched from the Beauchamp Tower to Cold Harbour Tower "to await his end in solitude." Seeing Sergeant Meryll, he asks Sir Richard Cholmondeley, Lieutenant of the Tower, for permission to greet him, and attempts to comfort his old comrade-in-arms and the weeping Phoebe by singing one of Gilbert and Sullivan's most meditatively lyrical ballads:

Is life a boon?
  If so, it must befall,
    That Death, whene'er he call,
Must call too soon.

(Seventeen years later, when a monument to Sullivan was erected in the Embankment Gardens near the Savoy, Gilbert suggested these lines for the inscription.)

At the end of the ballad Phoebe, still in tears, is led away by her father. Fairfax asks the Lieutenant if he might be married before his execution to ensure that his estate will not pass to the kinsman who falsely accused him of sorcery. The sympathetic Lieutenant agrees, and all march off.

As Phoebe spins, she sings:
"When maiden loves, she mopes apart,
  As owl mopes on a tree . . ."

There is a hullabaloo as a noisy rabble pursues a gaily caparisoned caravan belonging to Jack Point and Elsie Maynard, strolling players. The Jester and Elsie try to mollify the crowd with a rendition of "The Merryman and His Maid" ("I Have a Song to Sing, O!"), which foretells indeed the unhappy love story of the two players.

Opportunely, the Lieutenant and his Yeomen appear and disperse the unmannerly crowd. When the Lieutenant discovers that Elsie is not only unmarried but in need of money to help her ailing mother, he proposes her as the bride—of very short duration—to Fairfax, in return for which she will be paid "an hundred crowns":

> *For half an hour*
> *You'll be a wife,*
> *And then the dower*
> *Is yours for life.*

At which all assembled sing, "Temptation, oh, temptation . . ." Elsie is blindfolded (why, except for the exigencies of Gilbert's plot, we'll never know) and led by Wilfred Shadbolt into Cold Harbour Tower. Jack Point, whose wry wit appeals to the Lieutenant, is hired to be his jester.

In a short time we see Elsie led out of the Tower by Wilfred, who removes the bandage from her eyes. He thinks it "an odd freak, for a dying man and his confessor to be closeted alone with a strange singing girl. I would fain have espied them, but they stopped up the keyhole. *My* keyhole!"

Phoebe comes upon Wilfred as he is puzzling about this, while her father remains in the background, unobserved. True to her word, she goes to work on the Head Jailer, from whom she can get anything she wants, slyly slipping the bunch of keys from his waistband and passing them to her father.

"Thou art a most . . . delightful companion," she lies to Wilfred. "Thine anecdotes of the torture-chamber are the prettiest hearing." And to beguile him until she can replace his keys, she sings of a fantasied lover:

> *Were I thy bride,*
> *Then all the world beside*
> *Were not too wide*
> *To hold my wealth of love—*
> *Were I thy bride!*

The besotted jailer never notices her replacing the keys, and is still in an amorous daze when she saucily finishes her song with, "But then, of course, you see, /I'm not thy bride!"

The ruse works, and Fairfax—spirited out of his cell, clean-shaven and dressed in Yeoman's uniform—is introduced by Sergeant Meryll as his hero son. The other Yeomen welcome him with fulsome praise for his brave deeds, embarrassing Fairfax. "The tales that of my prowess are narrated/Have been prodigiously exaggerated!" he

Colonel Fairfax, with an escort of Yeomen, is taken to Cold Harbour Tower to await execution.

Wilfred tethers one of the Tower crows.

protests. Of course, this display of modesty simply calls forth even greater tributes, which in turn elicit further disclaimers.

An end to the escalation comes with Phoebe's appearance. She greets Fairfax as his sister, ''little Phoebe,'' and when he finally grasps the situation, he also grasps Phoebe and they embrace under the watchful eye of the Head Jailer. ''There are three thou mayst hug,'' Wilbur dictates sternly to Phoebe: ''Thy father and thy brother and—myself!''

The erstwhile prisoner and Phoebe delightedly exchange kisses and embraces as the bells of St. Peter's within the Tower walls begin to toll for the execution. The crowd enters Tower Green, the block is brought out, and the masked Headsman takes his place, swinging the terrible ax experimentally. The Yeomen of the Guard form up, and the Lieutenant tells off Fairfax/Leonard and two other Yeomen, who, with Wilfred, march into the Tower to bring the prisoner to execution.

The bell continues its ominous tolling at two-bar intervals; the dead march and chorus have a funereal grandeur; but the solemn rhythms are shattered when Fairfax and the two Yeomen burst out of the Tower to announce that the prisoner is not there. He has ''vanished into empty air!'' Wilfred, as Head Jailer, is held responsible and is put under arrest.

Elsie is appalled at Fairfax's disappearance. She says in an aside to Jack Point, ''Oh, woe is me!/I am his wife, and he is free!'' But Point angrily replies:

> . . . *woe is* me, *I rather think!*
> *Whate'er betide*
> *You are his bride,*
> *And I am left*
> *Alone—bereft!*

There is a frenzy of excitement as the Yeomen and populace rush off to hunt down the fugitive, leaving Elsie to faint in the disguised Fairfax's arms while the Headsman stands immobile at his block.

ACT II: *Tower Green. Moonlight.*
> *(Two days are supposed to elapse between Acts I and II.)*

TWO DAYS HAVE PASSED AND THE NOCTURNAL SCENE is dismal. The prisoner is still at large and Dame Carruthers ridicules the Yeomen: ''Warders are ye?/Whom do ye ward?''

Jack Point's spirits are so low that he must read his flat jests from a book of stale humor. Wilfred is dejected too. (How he got out of jail is one of the unexplained mysteries of Gilbert's plot, but no matter.) Here he is, listening to Jack Point's patter song on how to be a jester—which is Wilfred Shadbolt's secret ambition. In return for lessons in comedy, Wilfred will swear that he shot Fairfax as he was escaping across the river and that the prisoner sank and was seen no

Jack Point becomes the Lieutenant's jester, promising:
''I've jibe and joke/And quip and crank
For lowly folk/And men of rank.''

A downcast Phoebe learns that there is no reprieve for Colonel Fairfax: ''Poor gentleman! poor gentleman!''

more. That will make Elsie a widow, and available for Point to marry. The two men are gleeful at the bargain they've struck.

Meanwhile Fairfax, ''Free from his fetters grim,'' is melancholy about the fetters that still bind him— to an unknown bride. ''From the one I broke readily enough—how to break the other!'' The plot thickens when Fairfax is joined by Sergeant Meryll, his supposed father, and Dame Carruthers, who bustles up to give father and son a warning: Elsie Maynard, who has a liking for the son, is ''no girl. She's a married woman.''

Dame Carruthers and the women are scornful of the Warders—who have let Fairfax escape: ''Spite of ye all, he is free—he is free!''

"Tush, old lady—she's promised to Jack Point," the Sergeant quickly tells her.

"Tush in thy teeth, old man!" retorts the Dame. She and her niece Kate have been nursing Elsie since her fainting spell and have heard her talk in her sleep about her marriage to Fairfax. As for Elsie's marrying a man who had but an hour to live, "There be those who would marry but for a minute, rather than die old maids."

Sergeant Meryll in an aside mutters, "Aye, I know one of them!" and we suspect that he's the one who got away from Dame Carruthers in some long-past romance.

Aunt and niece, father, and purported son sing the lovely quartet:

Strange adventure! Maiden wedded
To a groom she's never seen—
Never, never, never seen!
Groom about to be beheaded,
In an hour on Tower Green!
Tower, Tower, Tower Green!

It is one of Sullivan's most felicitous madrigals, and music reviewers, praising it, called attention to the composer's "unrivalled" skill in handling this Early English form.

Fairfax is pleased to learn that his mysterious bride is "this winsome Elsie" and he determines to test her faithfulness. When he en-

Sergeant Meryll is in the clutches of Dame Carruthers, who knows "what it is to give my heart to one who will have none of it!"

counters Elsie, he, in the guise of Leonard Meryll, declares his love for her and presses his suit so ardently that she is forced to confess she has a husband—none other than Colonel Fairfax. When he begs her to be his anyhow, she remains loyal to her husband even though she does not love him. Just as Fairfax is about to tell Elsie the truth, a shot is heard, possibly fired from the wharf along the Thames.

Once again, as at the end of Act I, the stage is in turmoil with everyone rushing on. The chorus sings:

> *What danger is at hand?*
> *Let us understand*
> *What danger is at hand!*

Phoebe sadly learns that Fairfax loves Elsie. "Before I pretend to be sister to anybody again, I'll turn nun . . ."

The Lieutenant demands to know the truth about who fired the shot. Wilfred and Point sing a nervously contradictory duet describing what happened to the figure Wilfred saw "creeping"—but who, the Jester insists, "was crawling." He turned out to be Colonel Fairfax, they aver, but he dived into the river and was shot through the head by Wilfred.

> WIL. *Like a stone I saw him sinking—*
> POINT. *I should say a lump of lead.*
> WIL. *Like a stone, my boy, I said—*
> POINT. *Like a heavy lump of lead. . . .*
> WIL. *Anyhow, the man is dead,*
> *Whether stone or lump of lead!*

Point tries to comfort the weeping Elsie, but she reminds him that the man was her husband—"and had he not been, he was nevertheless a living man, and now he is dead; and so, by your leave, my tears may flow unchidden, Master Point."

Fairfax asks the Jester if he really saw all this, and Point blusters, "Aye, with both eyes at once." It is a bold-faced lie, and all present know it, save Elsie—though Point believes he has taken them all in. Fairfax mischievously asks if he saw the man's face, and when Point describes how ugly and villainous it was, Phoebe and Fairfax cannot contain their mirth. The Jester, not pleased with being laughed at when he isn't trying to be funny, mutters, " 'Tis ever thus with simple folk—an accepted wit has but to say 'Pass the mustard,' and they roar their ribs out!" (We can hear Gilbert's curmudgeonly voice speaking from experience here.)

Point now turns to Elsie and offers himself to her, naming all of his qualities as a merryman in order to captivate her. But Fairfax cuts him short with a lesson on the art of wooing—"A Man Who Would Woo a Fair Maid"—for which the Jester is pathetically grateful. By the end of the lesson, however, it is clear to Phoebe and Point that the teacher has succeeded in winning Elsie for himself.

Phoebe, who has loved the Colonel from the beginning, is in tears; the Jester is heartbroken; but the two lovers are blissful. Left alone with her sorrow, Phoebe continues to weep, and when Wilfred comes along to comfort her she blurts out that the man she loves is to marry Elsie Maynard, "the little pale fool."

Wilfred at last realizes that the man Phoebe loves is evidently not her brother Leonard, though she "fondled, and coddled, and kissed" him—and that he must be none other than Fairfax. To prevent the truth from getting out, Phoebe quickly agrees to become Wilfred's wife, for "there's no help for it! Thou art a very brute—but even brutes must marry, I suppose." And when the Jailer embraces her she responds with a heartfelt "Ugh!" But learning from the real Leonard Meryll that Fairfax has been reprieved and is now free and out of danger, Phoebe turns again to Wilfred. "Come—I

Phoebe, Elsie, and Dame Carruthers sing of their wedding day: " 'Tis said that joy in full perfection / Comes only once to womankind . . ."

TRAUBNER THEATRE COLLECTION

"Misery me, lackadaydee!
He sipped no sup, and he craved no crumb,
As he sighed for the love of a ladye!"

am thy Phoebe—thy very own—and we will be wed in a year—or two—or three, at the most," promises the unenthusiastic fiancée.

Sergeant Meryll is similarly trapped into a promise of marriage to Dame Carruthers as the price for her silence about his complicity in Fairfax's escape. She, Phoebe, and Elsie—who is dressed in bridal finery (she is prepared to marry her beloved "Leonard")—sing of women's "day of joy" that comes only once. At "other times, on close inspection/Some lurking bitter we shall find."

But Elsie's "day of joy" is shattered by the Lieutenant, who brings her the news that her husband lives and is free. Covering her face with her hands, she weeps for her adored Leonard to come and claim her. Colonel Fairfax, handsomely dressed, has arrived instead, to whom Elsie says, "Would I had died!/Sir I obey!/I am thy bride!" Then, for the first time she looks up at him and recognizes— Leonard!

They embrace blissfully, but one man's joy-day is another's "lurking bitter." Poor Jack Point sings a brokenhearted reprise of "The Merryman and His Maid":

> *For I have a song to sing, O!*
>   *It is sung to the moon*
>   *By a love-lorn loon,*
> *Who fled from the mocking throng, O!*

At song's end the Jester falls insensible at Elsie's feet.

The tradition has been to play this as a death scene, making *Yeomen* a tragic opera. But George Grossmith, the original Jack Point, was not cast in the tragic mold, and while he followed Gilbert's stage directions to "fall insensible," he used to wiggle his toes and wink comically while the curtain descended, permitting the audience to leave with a chuckle instead of a tear.

D'OYLY CARTE'S OPERA COMPANY

THE GONDOLIERS

BY W. S. GILBERT AND ARTHUR SULLIVAN

DAVID ALLEN & SONS, BELFAST & LONDON. (REGD DESIGN)

THE GONDOLIERS

OR THE KING OF BARATARIA

Although Arthur Sullivan believed *The Yeomen of the Guard* to be the best of the operas he wrote with Gilbert, it did not fulfill his aspirations "to do some more dramatic work on a larger musical scale." Not many months after *Yeomen* opened, Sullivan announced to D'Oyly Carte and then to Gilbert that in future works "the music must occupy a more important position than in our other pieces" and that he wanted "a voice in the *Musical* construction of the libretto." He invited Gilbert to collaborate with him on this next grand opera—"a major work of dramatic and serious purpose."

Flattering as the proposal must have appeared, coming from England's preeminent musical knight, it did not turn Gilbert's shrewd business head or distort his realistic self-appraisal. "We have a name, jointly, for humorous work," he wrote back to Sir Arthur, "tempered with occasional glimpses of earnest drama. I think we should do unwisely if we left, altogether, the path which we have trodden together so long and so successfully." Gilbert suggested that Sullivan should indeed write his big work. "But why abandon the Savoy business?" He then recommended the leading librettist of the time as a grand opera collaborator. "*My* work in that direction would be, deservedly or otherwise, generally pooh-poohed."

Sullivan, disappointed in the declining public interest in his favorite, *Yeomen,* after only five months, was loath to return to their "former style of piece" in pursuit of success: ". . . I cannot do it. I have lost the liking for writing Comic opera . . ." But his real objection was then flatly expressed: in all their comic operas Sullivan felt he had been forced to sacrifice himself; the music was subordinate to the words. Now he wanted to engage in a work in which "music is to be the first consideration—where words are to suggest music, not govern it . . ."

Gilbert, irascible at best, and now gout-ridden, waited a week before zapping back with his famous riposte expressing astonishment

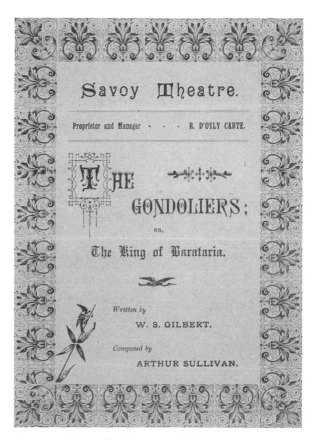

Program from the first run of The Gondoliers, *with D'Oyly Carte prominently billed as Proprietor and Manager of the Savoy.*

"From the sunny Spanish shore,/The Duke of Plaza-Tor!/ . . . His Grace's daughter . . ./And His Grace's private drum/To Venetia's shores have come . . ."

The Gondoliers *characters achieved commercial immortality on cigarette cards—now valuable collectibles.*

at Sullivan's impression of self-effacement during their twelve-year collaboration and the composer's present desire for the libretto—''& consequently the librettist''—to occupy a subordinate position: ''. . . then there is most certainly no *modus vivendi* to be found that shall be satisfactory to both of us. You are an adept at your profession & I am an adept in mine. If we meet, it must be as master & master— not as master & servant.''

A brilliant example of the firmly slammed door—that is yet left open a tiny crack!

Sullivan took advantage of the slight opening a few weeks later in a conciliatory letter that concretely outlined some not-unreasonable requests for his increased authority in certain musical situations. He had been vacationing with the Prince of Wales on the Mediterranean, as was his extravagant custom, and perhaps the desire to maintain this costly life-style, coupled with Carte's persuasive peacemaking a bit later in Paris, resulted in Sullivan's capitulation: ''. . . I am quite prepared to set to work at once upon a light or comic opera with you, (provided of course that we are thoroughly agreed about the subject) . . .''

On Sullivan's return to England in the spring, he and Gilbert had a frank discussion that cleared the air. ''Shook hands and buried the hatchet,'' the composer's diary relates.

D'Oyly Carte commissioned Sullivan to write a grand opera based on Sir Walter Scott's *Ivanhoe* for the opening of Carte's new Royal English Opera House the following year. With the opportunity

to create the serious musical work of his dreams, Sullivan's liking for writing comic opera was miraculously found again. And when he had his first inkling of the new idea, he wrote to Gilbert: "I understand from him [Carte] sometime ago that you had some subject connected with Venice & Venetian life, and this seemed to me to hold out great chances of bright colours and taking music. Can you not develop this into something we can both go into with warmth & enthusiasm . . . ?"

The two men worked from early June until early October on the numbers for their new opera, Gilbert sending the lyrics piecemeal for the composer to set. The libretto, a good-natured satire on the budding interest in social and political equality, took five months for Gilbert to write. Since of the forty-seven pages of libretto only fourteen were dialogue, Sullivan possibly got more music than he had bargained for, and complained that "There is a good deal more work in it than there was in *The Yeomen* for nearly all the numbers are rapid. . . . Of course the result is that there are more pages in the score. Two minutes *Allegro* means perhaps twenty pages, but with an *Andante* movement you would use only about six." None of Gilbert and Sullivan's previous operas involved such lengthy preparation; in none were librettist and composer so mutually considerate.

"*The Gondoliers* a Great Success," trumpeted the *Sunday Times* headline after the opening. But perhaps of greater significance to the Savoy triumvirate that had come safely through a time of personal conflict was the *Daily Telegraph*'s observation: "*The Gondoliers* conveys an impression of having been written *con amore*."

A little piazza in Venice, where Act I takes place.

The Gondoliers Waltz

On Airs from W.S. Gilbert & Arthur Sullivans Opera

by P. Bucalossi

LONDON CHAPPELL & Co. 50 NEW BOND STREET. W.
CITY BRANCH 15 POULTRY E.C.

PRICE 4/-
DUET 4/-
SEPTETT 1/-
FULL ORCHESTRA 2/-

THE GONDOLIERS

OR THE KING OF BARATARIA

ACT I: *The Piazzetta, Venice.*

THE CURTAIN RISES ON A LITTLE PIAZZA IN VENICE fronting on a small canal. A group of colorful contadine, or Venetian flower girls, are binding their white and red roses into bouquets and singing prettily:

> *List and learn, ye dainty roses,*
> > *Roses white and roses red,*
> *Why we bind you into posies*
> > *Ere your morning bloom has fled.*

The flowers will have to deliver their messages of love, since the girls themselves must appear to be indifferent: they all, it transpires, love the same young men, "peerless in their beauty," who are coming to choose their brides. But, alas, there are four-and-twenty contadine and only two young men!

As they sing, a group of gondoliers amble into the little square unobserved by the girls. And then the objects of the girls' affection arrive by gondola—the handsome Marco and Giuseppe. The girls load them down with their fresh bouquets and the two young men exclaim from behind armloads of flowers, "O ciel'!" and launch into their famous duet, "We're Called *Gondolieri.*" They then have handkerchiefs tied around their eyes so that, blindfolded, they may let fate choose their mates impartially from among the girls.

A charming game of blindman's buff ensues and eventually Marco catches the lovely Gianetta, while Giuseppe grabs the fair Tessa. "I've at length achieved a capture!" Giuseppe cries as he removes his blindfold: ". . . Rapture, rapture!" (Surely one of Gilbert's favorite exclamations.) And now, following fate's decree, the two happy couples hurry away to be married with all the contadine and gondoliers dancing off after them.

This opening sequence of song and recitative is the second-longest passage of music unbroken by spoken words in all of Gilbert

Dramatis Personae:

THE DUKE OF PLAZA-TORO, a Grandee of Spain (Baritone)

LUIZ, His Attendant (Tenor)

DON ALHAMBRA DEL BOLERO, the Grand Inquisitor (Bass-baritone)

MARCO PALMIERI (Tenor)
GIUSEPPE PALMIERI (Baritone)
ANTONIO
FRANCESCO } Venetian Gondoliers
GIORGIO
ANNIBALE

THE DUCHESS OF PLAZA-TORO (Contralto)

CASILDA, Her Daughter (Soprano)

GIANETTA (Soprano)
TESSA (Mezzo-soprano)
FIAMETTA } Contadine
VITTORIA
GIULIA

INEZ, the King's Foster-mother (Contralto)

Chorus of Gondoliers and Contadine, Men-at-Arms, Heralds, and Pages

TIME: *1750.*

First produced at the Savoy Theatre on December 7, 1889.

"Then turn us round—and we, with all convenient despatch,
Will undertake to marry any two of you we catch!"

and Sullivan, running for more than eighteen minutes. Sullivan at last was permitted to indulge his desire to compose in the true grand-opera style, and he played it to the hilt.

At this point comes a short musical introduction and a flourish. A gondola glides up to the Piazzetta landing, and out step the shabby Duke of Plazo-Toro, his duchess, their daughter Casilda, and their "suite"—an exaggerated description of their lone attendant, Luiz. Gilbert will begin to have some fun now with social pretensions and class distinctions as his broken-down Spanish Grandee and family illustrate the ridiculous affectations of snobbery.

"The young man seems to entertain but an imperfect appreciation of the respect due from a menial to a Castilian hidalgo," sneers Casilda when the "suite" neglects at first to kneel to the Duke. But Luiz has the grace to spare his employer's feelings by labeling the halberdiers who failed to meet him "mercenary" and the band of musicians who failed to escort him "sordid" for wanting payment in advance.

"But surely they know His Grace?" the Duchess exclaims.

"Exactly—they know His Grace," is Luiz's smooth reply.

The family has crossed the sea to demand an audience with the Grand Inquisitor. The Duke should have preferred to ride through the streets of Venice like a gentleman, on horseback; "but owing . . . to an unusually wet season," he observes, "the streets are in such a condition that equestrian exercise is impracticable."

The great secret the Duke now imparts to Casilda is that she was married when only six months old to the infant son and heir of the wealthy King of Barataria (the name of the island governed by Sancho Panza in Cervantes' *Don Quixote*). When the King became a Wesleyan Methodist "of the most bigoted and persecuting type," the Grand Inquisitor spirited the infant prince to Venice. Two weeks ago the Methodist monarch and his court were killed in an insurrection, and now the Duke wants to find his son-in-law, the new King, and he hails his daughter as "Her Majesty, the reigning Queen of Barataria!"

When a drum rolls and the Duke kneels before his royal daughter, that young woman exclaims: "I, the Queen of Barataria! But I've nothing to wear!"

Her father reassures her that the Duke of Plaza-Toro does not need to follow fashions; he *leads* them, as he even occasionally led his armies into action. And he swings into the song about his military methods:

In enterprise of martial kind,
    When there was any fighting,
He led his regiment from behind—
    He found it less exciting.

The Duke and his Duchess sweep off to the Grand Ducal Palace, and as soon as they have disappeared we are amazed to see the

"We're called gondolieri,
But that's a vagary,
It's quite honorary
    The trade that we ply."

haughty Casilda rush into the arms of Luiz, the lowly drummer-factotum who has borne the brunt of her insolence. They sing a love duet in which Casilda explains:

Ah, well-beloved,
Mine angry frown
Is but a gown
That serves to dress
My gentleness!

When Casilda tells Luiz that she has embraced him for the last time—for she has just discovered she was "wed in babyhood to the infant son of the King of Barataria!"—Luiz exclaims that his mother was the nurse to whose charge the baby was entrusted. Luiz and Casilda may not love now or in the future, but the past is irrevocably theirs, and they can continue to make love in the past tense. Luiz exclaims: ". . . my lately loved, my recently adored, tell me . . . I was all in all to thee!"

The Duke and Duchess emerge from the Ducal Palace followed by Don Alhambra del Bolero, the Grand Inquisitor of Spain, an imposing figure dressed in courtly black. "And a very nice little lady, too!" he pronounces upon being presented to Casilda. "Jimp, isn't she?" her doting father asks—and Gilbert introduces us to a word of Scandinavian origin meaning slim, slender, delicate, neat, graceful, which very likely was taken up by hip Victorian audiences when he sprang it on them, and which perfectly describes his ideal girl.

The Don tells them that the Prince, whom he stole and brought to Venice, was left with "a highly respectable gondolier," who had a son of the identical age. The Prince is here plying that same modest but picturesque calling. The gondolier meanwhile perished: "A taste for drink combined with gout,/Had doubled him up for ever." (Gout is not the only autobiographical note sounded in this passage. Gilbert as a two-year-old in Naples was handed over by his nurse to a couple of Italian rogues, who then held him for ransom. His father paid them £25 and young William later was returned safely.)

Casilda is distressed to learn that she is "married to one of two gondoliers . . . impossible to say which?"

But, bless my heart, consider my position!
I am the wife of one, that's very clear;
But who can tell, except by intuition,
Which is the Prince, and which the Gondolier?

The Grand Inquisitor, who is informed about everything and everyone, will send for Luiz's mother, whom he knows to have been the Prince's nurse, and have her establish the identity of the true King of Barataria.

The Duke and Duchess, Casilda, Luiz, and the Grand Inquisitor, after deciding that "Life's a pleasant institution,/Let us take it as it comes!" go their carefree ways, leaving the stage to the gondoliers, contadine, and the two newlywed couples.

"Gay and gallant gondolieri,
Take us both and hold us tightly,
You have luck extraordinary;
We might both have been unsightly!"

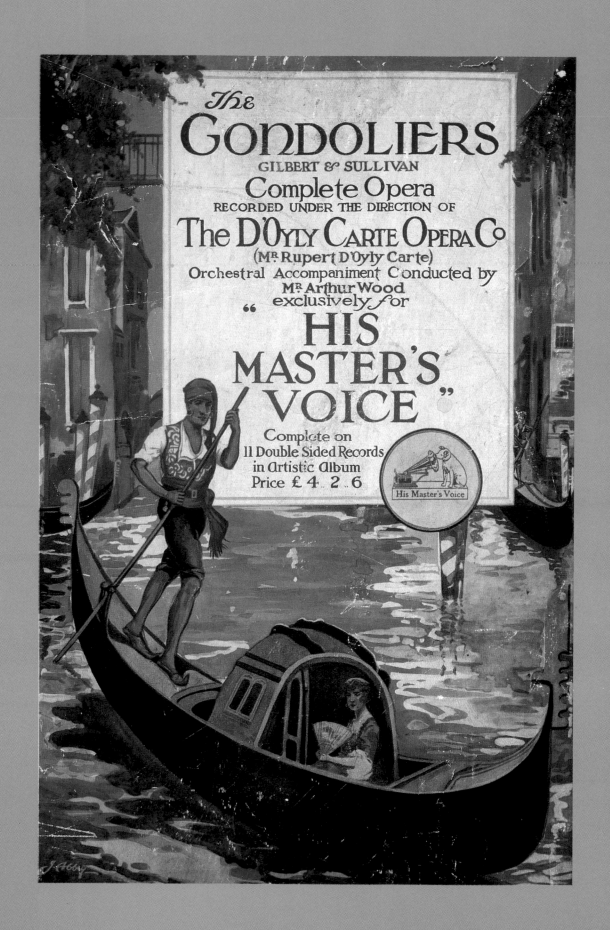

Don Alhambra, with a special interest in the gondoliers, returns to strike up a conversation with Giuseppe and Marco and their brides in an attempt to find out the ages of the two men. "We are jolly gondoliers," says Giuseppe staunchly, "the sons of Baptisto Palmieri, who led the last revolution. Republicans, heart and soul, we hold all men to be equal."

The Inquisitor drops his bombshell. "One of you may be Baptisto's son . . . but the other is no less a personage than the only son of the late King of Barataria."

The young men are astounded and distressed. "What does it matter?" asks the Inquisitor. "As you are both Republicans, and hold kings in detestation, of course you'll abdicate at once."

Giuseppe admits that "there are kings and kings. When I say that I detest kings," he backpedals, "I mean I detest *bad* kings." It is obvious that the possibility of his own kingship is very tempting to this heart-and-soul Republican!

Don Alhambra has little trouble persuading the two gondoliers to pack up a few belongings and quickly get to Barataria, where they will reign jointly until things are sorted out. Their brides will not be able to join them until later. The brides weep at being parted from their husbands after only half an hour but, cheered by the thought of their honeymoon reunion, Gianetta sings

> *Then one of us will be a Queen,*
> *And sit on a golden throne,*
> *With a crown instead*
> *Of a hat on her head,*
> *And diamonds all her own!*

Before they sail away, Giuseppe and Marco invite everyone to come to their kingdom, where "all shall equal be!"

> *The Earl, the Marquis, and the Dook,*
> *The Groom, the Butler, and the Cook . . .*

> *The Aristocrat who banks with Coutts—*
> *The Aristocrat who hunts and shoots—*
> *The Aristocrat who cleans our boots . . .*

Then, embracing their brides, they sail away to their "island fair/ That lies in a Southern sea."

Tessa sings to Giuseppe:
"When a merry maiden marries,
Sorrow goes and pleasure tarries;
Every sound becomes a song,
All is right, and nothing's wrong!"

ACT II: *Pavilion in the Palace of Barataria.*

(An interval of three months is supposed to elapse between Acts I and II.)

THREE MONTHS LATER, IN THE COURT OF BARATARIA, the two erstwhile gondoliers are magnificently dressed, seated on twin thrones. They are busy polishing the crown and scepter. Their fellow

A 1919 record album of Rupert D'Oyly Carte's production of The Gondoliers.

The vivacious fandango gave Victorian audiences a naughty flash of shapely legs.

"After sailing to this island—
Tossing in a manner frightful,
We are all once more on dry land—
And we find the change delightful . . ."

gondoliers, dressed as courtiers, officers, soldiers, and servants, are enjoying themselves at cards, dice, and other games—without regard for social distinctions. Singing of life in Barataria, they chorus:

> *This form of government we find*
> *The beau ideal of its kind—*
> *A despotism strict combined*
>   *With absolute equality!*

Marco and Giuseppe, justifying their kingly position, make themselves useful about the palace. They sing a song listing the duties of a Republican monarch that greatly amused Queen Victoria at a command performance at Windsor.

> *First, we polish off some batches*
> *Of political despatches,*
>   *And foreign politicians circumvent;*
> *Then, if business isn't heavy,*
> *We may hold a royal* levée,
>   *Or ratify some Acts of Parliament.*

It is a very pleasant life, except that they miss "the dear little wives [they] left behind." Marco's tenor aria, "Take a Pair of Sparkling Eyes," is one of the most popular songs in the Gilbert and Sullivan canon, giving as it does the "only . . . recipe for perfect happiness." When Marco sings the final note, as if magically summoned by the tender song the ladies burst in—the troupe of contadine and the two brides, who could stand the separation no longer.

To celebrate the happy reunion Giuseppe proposes a banquet and a dance. "A banquet *and* a dance! O, it's too much happiness!" cries Tessa, his rapturous bride. All break into a spirited song and dance:

> *Dance a cachucha, fandango, bolero,*
> *Xeres we'll drink—Manzanilla, Montero . . .*

Don Alhambra's sudden appearance cuts short the revelry. His snobbery is offended by the sight of footmen and grooms dancing with the gentry. When Giuseppe offers him some macaroni from the banquet, the Don has to turn it down because of his gout. (We can see Gilbert between the lines!) He tries to impress upon the inexperienced rulers why their Republican society will not work, singing a song with a moral about a king of old who promoted everybody, and which ends: "To this conclusion you'll agree,/When everyone is somebodee,/Then no one's anybody!" But he really distresses Marco and Giuseppe when he reveals that one of them was married to Casilda in infancy. Therefore, one of them is "an unintentional bigamist."

While the distraught young couples leave to try to find a solution to their dilemma, the noble strains of a processional are heard. In dignified and martial tread, lavishly costumed retainers herald the approach of the Duke of Plaza-Toro, his Duchess, and Casilda—all now dressed with the utmost magnificence.

The Duke demands an audience with the King of Barataria, "a double gentleman" who will "boil down to a single gentleman" when the circumstances are ascertained—"a unique example of an individual who becomes a single man and a married man by the same operation." The Duchess gives her daughter some advice on the ability to love one's husband, no matter what. "It was very difficult . . . but I said to myself, 'That man is a Duke, and I *will* love him.' " The Duchess's song recounts amusingly how she tamed Casilda's progenitor.

The Duke, who has incorporated himself, has a bit of business advice that he and his Duchess present, winding up pragmatically:

"I am now about to address myself to the gentleman whom my daughter married; the other may allow his attention to wander . . ."

In short, if you'd kindle
The spark of a swindle
 Lure simpletons into your clutches . . .

Or hoodwink a debtor,
You cannot do better
 Than trot out a Duke or a Duchess . . .

When Marco and Giuseppe, the "double gentleman," appear
they are given a hilarious lesson in courtly manners and style by the
ducal couple, who dance a stately gavotte with the two suitors and
their daughter, and then dance off. "The old birds have gone away
and left the young chickens together. That's called tact,"
Giuseppe observes.

Costume designs for Rupert
D'Oyly Carte's lavish
twentieth-century production
of The Gondoliers.

The young people are honest with one another, Casilda confessing she is "over head and ears in love with somebody else," while Giuseppe and Marco, suddenly joined by their wives, explain that they are already married. It seems they are all faced with "a profound catastrophe."

At this complicated juncture Don Alhambra, the Duke and Duchess, and all the others return. The Don brings forward Inez, foster mother of the Prince, who will tell them which young man is the rightful king, thanks to the prodding of the Grand Inquisitor's torture chamber.

Don Alhambra, the Grand Inquisitor, announces: "Now let the loyal lieges gather round—/The Prince's foster-mother has been found!"

"This polite attention touches
Heart of Duke and heart of Duchess,
*   Who resign their pet*
*   With profound regret."*

"Is this indeed the King?
  Oh, wondrous revelation!
Oh, unexpected thing!
  Unlooked-for situation!"

Inez, in eight lines, unravels all the complications of the plot by announcing that when traitors came to steal the Prince entrusted to her by the King, she deftly substituted her own son, and kept the real Prince, whom she then called "son." So Luiz, her "son," is really His Royal Highness. A sensation! Crowned and robed, he ascends the throne as King. Casilda rushes to his arms.

Marco, Gianetta, Giuseppe, and Tessa are, on the whole, delighted, though they admit to "sentiments conflicting."

Gilbert's libretto ended with:

Then hail, O King of a Golden Land,
And the high-born bride who claims his hand!
The past is dead, and you gain your own,
A royal crown and a golden throne!

Deferring to Sullivan's decision on how to end the opera on the most exuberant note, Gilbert agreed to a reprise of "We're Called *Gondolieri*" and of the lively cachucha. We leave *The Gondoliers* "with feelings of pleasure," as the entire company is spinning and stamping and twirling madly.

"The attractions of *The Gondoliers* are numerous," said the *Topical Times* review; "the chorus wore comparatively short skirts for the first time, and the gratifying fact is revealed to a curious world that the Savoy chorus are a very well-legged lot."

Ah, innocent Victorians!

CASTS AND CREDITS FOR THE TELEVISION PRODUCTIONS

THE BEST-LOVED TEAM of librettist and composer in the history of comic opera surely warrant special attention from the young medium of television. And that is what Gilbert and Sullivan receive in Brent Walker's definitive television festival of their operas. With the most talented creative and technical people from film, television, the stage, and opera to back them up, Emmy Award–winning producer Judith de Paul and Executive Producer and financier George Walker assembled an exciting international cast in which stars from both sides of the Atlantic and all branches of the theatrical arts mingled.

Without sacrificing the traditional qualities of the operas, this unique series is a major collaborative effort in which new approaches to the productions were conceived with the television camera and screen in mind. The vitality of Gilbert and Sullivan in this new medium is apparent in the lively production scenes that illustrate this book.

The London Symphony Orchestra, conducted by Alexander Faris, and the Ambrosian Opera chorus under chorus master John McCarthy, capture the elegance, wit, and charm of Sullivan's music and Gilbert's lyrics. The casts and credits for the twelve operas follow.

FOR ALL THE OPERAS

Executive Producer: George Walker
Producer: Judith de Paul
Production Designer: Allan Cameron
Lighting Designer: Paul Beeson
Costume Designer: Jenny Beavan
Choreographer: Terry Gilbert

COX AND BOX

CAST

Cox: Russell Smythe
Box: John Fryatt
Sergeant Bouncer, Landlord: Tom Lawlor

CREDITS

Camera Director: Dave Heather
Stage Producer: David Alden

TRIAL BY JURY

CAST

The Learned Judge: Frankie Howerd
The Plaintiff: Kate Flowers
The Defendant: Ryland Davies
Counsel for the Plaintiff: Tom McDonnell
Usher: Roger Bryson
Foreman of the Jury: Brian Donlan
First Bridesmaid: Elise McDougall

CREDITS

Camera Director: Derek Bailey
Stage Producer: Wendy Toye

THE SORCERER

CAST

John Wellington Wells: Clive Revill
Dr. Daly: David Kernan
Sir Marmaduke Pointdextre: Donald Adams
Alexis: Alexander Oliver
Lady Sangazure: Nuala Willis
Aline: Nan Christie
Mrs. Partlett: Enid Hartle
Constance: Janis Kelly

CREDITS

Camera Director: Dave Heather
Stage Producer: Stephen Pimlott

H.M.S. PINAFORE

CAST

Captain Corcoran: Peter Marshall
Sir Joseph Porter: Frankie Howerd
Josephine: Meryl Drower
Ralph Rackstraw: Michael Bulman
Buttercup: Della Jones
Hebe: Anne Mason
Dick Deadeye: Alan Watt
Boatswain: Gordon Sandison

CREDITS

Camera Director: Rodney Greenberg
Stage Producer: Michael Geliot

THE PIRATES OF PENZANCE

CAST

The Pirate King: Peter Allen
Major-General Stanley: Keith Michell
Frederic: Alexander Oliver
Mabel: Janis Kelly
Ruth: Gillian Knight
Sergeant of Police: Paul Hudson
Edith: Kate Flowers
Kate: Jenny Wren
Samuel: Brian Donlan

CREDITS

Camera Director: Rodney Greenberg
Stage Producer: Michael Geliot

PATIENCE

CAST

Reginald Bunthorne: Derek Hammond-Stroud
Archibald Grosvenor: John Fryatt
Colonel Calverley: Donald Adams
Major Murgatroyd: Roderick Kennedy
The Duke of Dunstable: Terry Jenkins
Lady Angela: Shirley Chapman
Lady Saphir: Shelagh Squires
Lady Ella: Patricia Hay
Lady Jane: Anne Collins
Patience: Sandra Dugdale

CREDITS

Camera Director: Dave Heather
Stage Producer: John Cox

IOLANTHE

CAST

The Lord Chancellor: Derek Hammond-Stroud
Private Willis: Richard Van Allen
Strephon: Alexander Oliver
Phyllis: Kate Flowers
Earl of Mountararat: Thomas Hemsley
Earl Tolloller: David Hillman
Queen of the Fairies: Anne Collins
Iolanthe: Beverley Mills
Celia: Sandra Dugdale
Leila: Pamela Field

CREDITS

Camera Director: Dave Heather
Stage Producer: David Pountney

PRINCESS IDA

CAST

King Gama: Frank Gorshin
Princess Ida: Nan Christie
King Hildebrand: Neil Howlett
Hilarion: Laurence Dale
Cyril: Bernard Dickerson
Florian: Richard Jackson
Arac: Tano Rea
Guron: Peter Savidge
Scynthius: Christopher Booth-Jones
Lady Blanche: Anne Collins
Lady Psyche: Josephine Gordon
Melissa: Claire Powell
Sacharissa: Jenny Wren
Chloe: Elise McDougall

CREDITS

Camera Director: Dave Heather
Stage Producer: Terry Gilbert

THE MIKADO

CAST

The Mikado of Japan: William Conrad
Ko-Ko: Clive Revill
Pooh-Bah: Stafford Dean
Nanki-Poo: John Stewart
Yum-Yum: Kate Flowers
Katisha: Anne Collins
Pish-Tush: Gordon Sandison
Peep-Bo: Fiona Dobie
Pitti-Sing: Cynthia Buchan

Camera Director: Rodney Greenberg
Stage Producer: Michael Geliot

RUDDIGORE

CAST

Sir Despard Murgatroyd: Vincent Price
Robin Oakapple: Keith Michell
Richard Dauntless: John Treleaven
Sir Roderic Murgatroyd: Donald Adams
Old Adam Goodheart: Paul Hudson
Rose Maybud: Sandra Dugdale
Mad Margaret: Ann Howard
Dame Hannah: Johanna Peters
Zorah: Beryl Korman
Ruth: Elise McDougall

CREDITS

Camera Director: Barrie Gavin
Stage Producer: Christopher Renshaw

THE YEOMEN OF THE GUARD

CAST

Jack Point: Joel Grey
Wilfred Shadbolt: Alfred Marks
Elsie Maynard: Elizabeth Gale
Colonel Fairfax: David Hillman

Dame Carruthers: Elizabeth Bainbridge
Sir Richard Cholmondeley: Peter Savidge
Sergeant Meryll: Geoffrey Chard
Leonard Meryll: Michael Bulman
Phoebe Meryll: Claire Powell
Kate: Beryl Korman

CREDITS

Camera Director: Dave Heather
Stage Producer: Anthony Besch

THE GONDOLIERS

CAST

Don Alhambra del Bolero: Keith Michell
The Duke of Plaza-Toro: Eric Shilling
Marco Palmieri: Francis Egerton
Giuseppe Palmieri: Tom McDonnell
The Duchess of Plaza-Toro: Anne Collins
Gianetta: Nan Christie
Casilda: Sandra Dugdale
Tessa: Fiona Kimm
Luiz: Christopher Booth-Jones

CREDITS

Camera Director: Dave Heather
Stage Producer: Peter Wood

All still photographs of the television productions are by Nick Fogden.

A SAMPLER OF SONG LYRICS

FROM THE OPERAS

COX AND BOX

Box's Lullaby

Hushed is the bacon on the grid,
I'll take a nap and close my eye,
Soon shall I be nodding, nodding nid,
Nid, nodding, nodding, nodding, nodding,
Singing lullaby, lullaby, lullaby,
Lulla, lulla, lulla, lulla, lullaby.
Hush-a-bye, bacon, on the coal top,
Till I awaken, there you will stop,
Lullaby, lullaby.

TRIAL BY JURY

The Defendant's Song

When first my old, old love I knew,
  My bosom welled with joy;
My riches at her feet I threw—
  I was a love-sick boy!
No terms seemed too extravagant
  Upon her to employ—
I used to mope, and sigh, and pant,
  Just like a love-sick boy!
    Tink-a-Tank—Tink-a-Tank.

But joy incessant palls the sense;
  And love, unchanged, will cloy,
And she became a bore intense
  Unto her love-sick boy!
With fitful glimmer burnt my flame,
  And I grew cold and coy,
At last, one morning, I became
  Another's love-sick boy.
    Tink-a-Tank—Tink-a-Tank.

The Judge's Song

When I, good friends, was called to the bar,
  I'd an appetite fresh and hearty,
But I was, as many young barristers are,
  An impecunious party.
I'd a swallow-tail coat of a beautiful blue—
  A brief which I bought of a booby
A couple of shirts and a collar or two,
  And a ring that looked like a ruby!

In Westminster Hall I danced a dance,
  Like a semi-despondent fury;
For I thought I should never hit on a chance
  Of addressing a British Jury—
But I soon got tired of third-class journeys,
  And dinners of bread and water;
So I fell in love with a rich attorney's
  Elderly, ugly daughter.

The rich attorney, he jumped with joy,
  And replied to my fond professions:
"You shall reap the reward of your pluck, my boy
  At the Bailey and Middlesex Sessions.
You'll soon get used to her looks," said he,
  "And a very nice girl you'll find her!
She may very well pass for forty-three
  In the dusk, with a light behind her!"

The rich attorney was good as his word;
  The briefs came trooping gaily,
And every day my voice was heard
  At the Sessions or Ancient Bailey.
All thieves who could my fees afford
  Relied on my orations,
And many a burglar I've restored
  To his friends and his relations.

At length I became as rich as the Gurneys—
  An incubus then I thought her,
So I threw over that rich attorney's
  Elderly, ugly daughter.

The rich attorney my character high
  Tried vainly to disparage—
And now, if you please, I'm ready to try
  This Breach of Promise of Marriage!

THE SORCERER

The Curate's Ballad

Time was when Love and I were well acquainted.
  Time was when we walked ever hand in hand.
A saintly youth, with worldly thought untainted,
  None better-loved than I in all the land!
Time was, when maidens of the noblest station,
  Forsaking even military men,
Would gaze upon me, rapt in adoration—
  Ah me, I was a fair young curate then!

Had I a headache? sighed the maids assembled;
  Had I a cold? welled forth the silent tear;
Did I look pale? then half a parish trembled;
  And when I coughed all thought the end was near!
I had no care—no jealous doubts hung o'er me—
  For I was loved beyond all other men.
Fled gilded dukes and belted earls before me—
  Ah me, I was a pale young curate then!

Alexis's Ballad

Love feeds on many kinds of food, I know,
  Some love for rank, and some for duty:
Some give their hearts away for empty show,
  And others love for youth and beauty.
To love for money all the world is prone:
  Some love themselves, and live all lonely:
Give me the love that loves for love alone—
  I love that love—I love it only!

What man for any other joy can thirst,
  Whose loving wife adores him duly?
Want, misery, and care may do their worst,
  If loving woman loves you truly.
A lover's thoughts are ever with his own—
  None truly loved is ever lonely:
Give me the love that loves for love alone—
  I love that love—I love it only!

The Tea-cup Brindisi
(Sir Marmaduke and Dr. Daly)

Eat, drink, and be gay,
  Banish all worry and sorrow,
Laugh gaily to-day,
  Weep, if you're sorry, to-morrow!
Come, pass the cup round—
  I will go bail for the liquor;
It's strong, I'll be bound,
  For it was brewed by the vicar!

Pain, trouble, and care,
  Misery, heart-ache, and worry,
Quick, out of your lair!
  Get you all gone in a hurry!
Toil, sorrow, and plot,
  Fly away quicker and quicker—
Three spoons to the pot—
  That is the brew of your vicar!

H.M.S. PINAFORE

Glee
(Ralph, Boatswain, Boatswain's Mate)

A British tar is a soaring soul,
  As free as a mountain bird,
His energetic fist should be ready to resist
  A dictatorial word.
His nose should pant and his lip should curl,
His cheeks should flame and his brow should furl,
His bosom should heave and his heart should glow,
And his fist be ever ready for a knock-down blow.

His eyes should flash with an inborn fire,
  His brow with scorn be wrung;
He never should bow down to a domineering frown,
  Or the tang of a tyrant tongue.
His foot should stamp and his throat should growl,
His hair should twirl and his face should scowl;
His eyes should flash and his breast protrude,
And this should be his customary attitude—[pose].

Sir Joseph's Song

When I was a lad I served a term
As office boy to an Attorney's firm.
I cleaned the windows and I swept the floor,
And I polished up the handle of the big front door.
  I polished up that handle so carefullee
  That now I am the Ruler of the Queen's Navee!

As office boy I made such a mark
That they gave me the post of a junior clerk.
I served the writs with a smile so bland,
And I copied all the letters in a big round hand—
  I copied all the letters in a hand so free,
  That now I am the Ruler of the Queen's Navee!

In serving writs I made such a name
That an articled clerk I soon became;
I wore clean collars and a brand-new suit
For the pass examination at the Institute,
  And that pass examination did so well for me,
  That now I am the Ruler of the Queen's Navee!

Of legal knowledge I acquired such a grip
That they took me into the partnership.
And that junior partnership, I ween,

Was the only ship that I ever had seen.
  But that kind of ship so suited me,
    That now I am the Ruler of the Queen's Navee!

I grew so rich that I was sent
By a pocket borough into Parliament.
I always voted at my party's call,
And I never thought of thinking for myself at all.
  I thought so little, they rewarded me
    By making me the Ruler of the Queen's Navee!

Now landsmen all, whoever you may be,
If you want to rise to the top of the tree,
If your soul isn't fettered to an office stool,
Be careful to be guided by this golden rule—
  Stick close to your desks and never go to sea,
    And you all may be Rulers of the Queen's Navee!

Captain Corcoran's Song

Fair moon, to thee I sing,
  Bright regent of the heavens,
Say, why is everything
  Either at sixes or at sevens?
I have lived hitherto
  Free from breath of slander,
Beloved by all my crew—
  A really popular commander.
But now my kindly crew rebel,
  My daughter to a tar is partial,
Sir Joseph storms, and, sad to tell,
  He threatens a court martial!
    Fair moon, to thee I sing,
      Bright regent of the heavens,
    Say, why is everything
      Either at sixes or at sevens?

THE PIRATES OF PENZANCE

The Pirate King's Song

Oh better far to live and die
Under the brave black flag I fly,
Than play a sanctimonious part,
With a pirate head and a pirate heart.
Away to the cheating world go you,
Where pirates all are well-to-do;
But I'll be true to the song I sing,
And live and die a Pirate King.
  For I am a Pirate King.

When I sally forth to seek my prey
I help myself in a royal way:
I sink a few more ships, it's true,
Than a well-bred monarch ought to do;
But many a king on a first-class throne,
If he wants to call his crown his own,

Must manage somehow to get through
More dirty work than ever *I* do,
  Though I am a Pirate King.

Frederick's Song

Oh, is there not one maiden breast
  Which does not feel the moral beauty
Of making worldy interest
  Subordinate to sense of duty?
Who would not give up willingly
  All matrimonial ambition,
To rescue such a one as I
  From his unfortunate position?

Oh, is there not one maiden here
  Whose homely face and bad complexion
Have caused all hopes to disappear
  Of ever winning man's affection?
To such a one, if such there be,
  I swear by Heaven's arch above you,
If you will cast your eyes on me—
  However plain you be—I'll love you!

The Sergeant's Song

When a felon's not engaged in his employment—
Or maturing his felonious little plans—
His capacity for innocent enjoyment—
Is just as great as any honest man's—
Our feelings we with difficulty smother
When constabulary duty's to be done
Ah, take one consideration with another—
A policeman's lot is not a happy one.

When the enterprising burglar's not a-burgling—
When the cut-throat isn't occupied in crime—
He loves to hear the little brook a-gurgling—
And listen to the merry village chime—
When the coster's finished jumping on his mother—
He loves to lie a-basking in the sun—
Ah, take one consideration with another—
The policeman's lot is not a happy one.

PATIENCE

The Love-sick Maidens' Song

Twenty love-sick maidens we,
  Love-sick all against our will.
Twenty years hence we shall be
  Twenty love-sick maidens still.
Twenty love-sick maidens we,
And we die for love of thee.

All our love is all for one,
  Yet that love he heedeth not.
He is coy and cares for none,
  Sad and sorry is our lot!
    Ah, miserie!

Colonel Calverley's Song

If you want a receipt for that popular mystery,
  Known to the world as a Heavy Dragoon,
Take all the remarkable people in history,
  Rattle them off to a popular tune.
The pluck of Lord Nelson on board of the *Victory*—
  Genius of Bismarck devising a plan—
The humour of Fielding (which sounds contradictory)—
  Coolness of Paget about to trepan—
The science of Jullien, the eminent musico—
  Wit of Macaulay, who wrote of Queen Anne—
The pathos of Paddy, as rendered by Boucicault—
  Style of the Bishop of Sodor and Man—
The dash of a D'Orsay, divested of quackery—
Narrative powers of Dickens and Thackeray—
Victor Emmanuel—peak-haunting Peveril—
Thomas Aquinas, and Doctor Sacheverell—
  Tupper and Tennyson—Daniel Defoe—
  Anthony Trollope and Mr. Guizot!
    Take of these elements all that is fusible,
    Melt them all down in a pipkin or crucible,
    Set them to simmer and take off the scum,
    And a Heavy Dragoon is the residuum!

Patience and Grosvenor's Duet

Prithee, pretty maiden—prithee, tell me true,
  (Hey, but I'm doleful, willow willow waly!)
Have you e'er a lover a-dangling after you?
    Hey willow waly O!
      I would fain discover
      If you have a lover?
    Hey willow waly O!

Gentle sir, my heart is frolicsome and free—
  (Hey, but he's doleful, willow willow waly!)
Nobody I care for comes a-courting me—
    Hey willow waly O!
      Nobody I care for
      Comes a-courting—therefore,
    Hey willow waly O!

Prithee, pretty maiden, will you marry me?
  (Hey, but I'm hopeful, willow willow waly!)
I may say, at once, I'm a man of propertee—
    Hey willow waly O!
      Money, I despise it;
      Many people prize it,
    Hey willow waly O!

Gentle sir, although to marry I design—
  (Hey, but he's hopeful, willow willow waly!)
As yet I do not know you, and so I must decline.

Hey willow waly O!
  To other maidens go you—
  As yet I do not know you,
Hey willow waly O!

Jane's Song

Silvered is the raven hair,
  Spreading is the parting straight,
Mottled the complexion fair,
  Halting is the youthful gait,
Hollow is the laughter free,
  Spectacled the limpid eye—
Little will be left of me
  In the coming by and by!

Fading is the taper waist,
  Shapeless grows the shapely limb
And although severely laced,
  Spreading is the figure trim!
Stouter than I used to be,
  Still more corpulent grow I—
There will be too much of me
  In the coming by and by!

IOLANTHE

Phyllis's Song

Good morrow, good lover!
  Good lover, good morrow!
I prithee discover,
    Steal, purchase, or borrow
      Some means of concealing
      The care you are feeling,
      And join in a measure
      Expressive of pleasure,
For we're to be married to-day—to-day!
  For we're to be married to-day!

The Lord Chancellor's Song

The Law is the true embodiment
Of everything that's excellent.
It has no kind of fault or flaw,
And I, my Lords, embody the Law.
The constitutional guardian I
Of pretty young Wards in Chancery,
All very agreeable girls—and none
Are over the age of twenty-one.
  A pleasant occupation for
  A rather susceptible Chancellor!

But though the compliment implied
Inflates me with legitimate pride,
It nevertheless can't be denied
That it has its inconvenient side.
For I'm not so old, and not so plain,

And I'm quite prepared to marry again,
But there'd be the deuce to pay in the Lords
If I fell in love with one of my Wards!
    Which rather tries my temper, for
    I'm *such* a susceptible Chancellor!

And every one who'd marry a Ward
Must come to me for my accord,
And in my court I sit all day,
Giving agreeable girls away,
With one for him—and one for he—
And one for you—and one for ye—
And one for thou—and one for thee—
But never, oh, never a one for me!
    Which is exasperating for
    A highly susceptible Chancellor!

Lord Tolloller's Ballad

Spurn not the nobly born
        With love affected,
Nor treat with virtuous scorn
        The well-connected.
High rank involves no shame—
We boast an equal claim
With him of humble name
        To be respected!
Blue blood! blue blood!
        When virtuous love is sought
        Thy power is naught,
Though dating from the Flood,
        Blue blood!

Spare us the bitter pain
        Of stern denials,
Nor with low-born disdain
        Augment our trials.
Hearts just as pure and fair
May beat in Belgrave Square
As in the lowly air
        Of Seven Dials!
Blue blood! Blue blood!
        Of what avail art thou
        To serve us now?
Though dating from the Flood,
        Blue blood!

Lord Mountararat's Song

When Britain really ruled the waves—
    (In good Queen Bess's time)
The House of Peers made no pretence
To intellectual eminence,
    Or scholarship sublime;
Yet Britain won her proudest bays
In good Queen Bess's glorious days!

When Wellington thrashed Bonaparte,
    As every child can tell,

The House of Peers, throughout the war,
Did nothing in particular,
    And did it very well:
Yet Britain set the world ablaze
In good King George's glorious days!

And while the House of Peers withholds
    Its legislative hand,
And noble statesmen do not itch
To interfere with matters which
    They do not understand,
As bright will shine Great Britain's rays
As in King George's glorious days!

PRINCESS IDA

Arac's Song

We are warriors three,
    Sons of Gama, Rex.
Like most sons are we,
    Masculine in sex.

Politics we bar,
    They are not our bent;
On the whole we are
    Not intelligent.

But with doughty heart,
    And with trusty blade
We can play our part—
    Fighting is our trade.

King Gama's Song

If you give me your attention, I will tell you what I am:
I'm a genuine philanthropist—all other kinds are sham.
Each little fault of temper and each social defect
In my erring fellow-creatures I endeavour to correct.
To all their little weaknesses I open people's eyes;
And little plans to snub the self-sufficient I devise;
I love my fellow-creatures—I do all the good I can—
Yet everybody says I'm such a disagreeable man!
        And I can't think why!

To compliments inflated I've a withering reply;
And vanity I always do my best to mortify;
A charitable action I can skilfully dissect;
And interested motives I'm delighted to detect;
I know everybody's income and what everybody earns;
And I carefully compare it with the income tax returns;
But to benefit humanity however much I plan,
Yet everybody says I'm such a disagreeable man!
        And I can't think why!

I'm sure I'm no ascetic; I'm as pleasant as can be;
You'll always find me ready with a crushing repartee.
I've an irritating chuckle, I've a celebrated sneer,

I've an entertaining snigger, I've a fascinating leer.
To everybody's prejudice I know a thing or two;
I can tell a woman's age in half a minute—and I do.
But although I try to make myself as pleasant as I can,
Yet everybody says I am a disagreeable man!
     And I can't think why!

Psyche's Song

If you'd climb the Helicon,
You should read Anacreon,
Ovid's *Metamorphoses,*
Likewise Aristophanes,
And the works of Juvenal:
These are worth attention, all;
But, if you will be advised,
You will get them Bowdlerized!

Cyril's Song

Would you know the kind of maid
  Sets my heart aflame-a?
Eyes must be downcast and staid,
  Cheeks must flush for shame-a!
    She may neither dance nor sing,
    But, demure in everything,
    Hang her head in modest way,
    With pouting lips that seem to say,
"Oh, kiss me, kiss me, kiss me, kiss me,
    Though I die of shame-a!"
Please you, that's the kind of maid
  Sets my heart aflame-a!

When a maid is bold and gay
  With a tongue goes clang-a,
Flaunting it in brave array,
  Maiden may go hang-a!
    Sunflower gay and hollyhock
    Never shall my garden stock;
    Mine the blushing rose of May,
    With pouting lips that seem to say,
"Oh, kiss me, kiss me, kiss me, kiss me,
    Though I die for shame-a!"
Please you, that's the kind of maid
  Sets my heart aflame-a!

Warriors' Song
(Arac, with Guron and Scynthius)

This helmet, I suppose,
Was meant to ward off blows,
  It's very hot,
  And weighs a lot,
As many a guardsman knows,
So off that helmet goes.

    Yes, yes, yes,
So off that helmet goes!

This tight-fitting cuirass
Is but a useless mass,
  It's made of steel,
  And weighs a deal,
A man is but an ass
Who fights in a cuirass,
So off goes that cuirass.

    Yes, yes, yes,
So off goes that cuirass!

These brassets, truth to tell,
May look uncommon well,
  But in a fight
  They're much too tight,
They're like a lobster shell!

    Yes, yes, yes,
They're like a lobster shell.

These things I treat the same,
(I quite forget their name.)
  They turn one's legs
  To cribbage pegs—
Their aid I thus disclaim,
Though I forget their name!

    Yes, yes, yes,
Their aid we thus disclaim!

THE MIKADO

Chorus of Nobles

If you want to know who we are,
  We are gentlemen of Japan;
On many a vase and jar—
  On many a screen and fan,
    We figure in lively paint:
    Our attitude's queer and quaint—
    You're wrong if you think it ain't, oh!

If you think we are worked by strings,
  Like a Japanese marionette,
You don't understand these things:
  It is simply Court etiquette.
    Perhaps you suppose this throng
    Can't keep it up all day long?
    If that's your idea, you're wrong, oh!

Chorus of Japanese Maidens

Braid the raven hair—
  Weave the supple tress—
Deck the maiden fair,
  In her loveliness—
Paint the pretty face—
  Dye the coral lip—

Emphasize the grace
    Of her ladyship!
Art and nature, thus allied,
Go to make a pretty bride.

Nanki-Poo and Ko-Ko's Duet

The flowers that bloom in the spring,
        Tra la,
    Breathe promise of merry sunshine—
As we merrily dance and we sing,
        Tra la,
We welcome the hope that they bring,
        Tra la,
    Of a summer of roses and wine.
        And that's what we mean when we say that a thing
        Is welcome as flowers that bloom in the spring.
            Tra la la la la la la, etc.

The flowers that bloom in the spring,
        Tra la,
    Have nothing to do with the case.
I've got to take under my wing,
        Tra la,
A most unattractive old thing,
        Tra la,
    With a caricature of a face
        And that's what I mean when I say, or I sing,
        "Oh, bother the flowers that bloom in the spring."
            Tra la la la la la, etc.

Ko-Ko's Song

On a tree by a river a little tom-tit
        Sang "Willow, titwillow, titwillow!"
And I said to him, "Dicky-bird, why do you sit
        Singing 'Willow, titwillow, titwillow'?"
"Is it weakness of intellect, birdie?" I cried,
"Or a rather tough worm in your little inside?"
With a shake of his poor little head, he replied,
        "Oh, willow, titwillow, titwillow!"

He slapped at his chest, as he sat on that bough,
        Singing "Willow, titwillow, titwillow!"
And a cold perspiration bespangled his brow,
        Oh, willow, titwillow, titwillow!
He sobbed and he sighed, and a gurgle he gave,
Then he plunged himself into the billowy wave,
And an echo arose from the suicide's grave—
        "Oh, willow, titwillow, titwillow!"

Now I feel just as sure as I'm sure that my name
        Isn't Willow, titwillow, titwillow,
That 'twas blighted affection that made him exclaim
        "Oh, willow, titwillow, titwillow!"
And if you remain callous and obdurate, I
Shall perish as he did, and you will know why,
Though I probably shall not exclaim as I die,
        "Oh, willow, titwillow, titwillow!"

RUDDIGORE

Chorus of Bridesmaids

Fair is Rose as bright May-day;
    Soft is Rose as warm west-wind;
Sweet is Rose as new-mown hay—
    Rose is queen of maiden-kind!
        Rose, all glowing
            With virgin blushes, say—
        Is anybody going
            To marry you to-day?

Chorus of Bucks and Blades and Bridesmaids

    When thoroughly tired
    Of being admired
By ladies of gentle degree—degree,
    With flattery sated,
    High-flown and inflated,
Away from the city we flee—we flee!
    From charms intramural
    To prettiness rural
    The sudden transition
    Is simply Elysian,
    So come, Amaryllis,
    Come, Chloe and Phyllis,
Your slaves, for the moment, are we!

    The sons of the tillage
    Who dwell in this village
Are people of lowly degree—degree.
    Though honest and active,
    They're most unattractive,
And awkward as awkward can be—can be.
    They're clumsy clodhoppers
    With axes and choppers,
    And shepherds and ploughmen
    And drovers and cowmen
    And hedgers and reapers
    And carters and keepers,
And never a lover for me!

Dame Hannah's Ballad

There grew a little flower
        'Neath a great oak tree:
When the tempest 'gan to lower
        Little heeded she:
No need had she to cower,
For she dreaded not its power—
She was happy in the bower
        Of her great oak tree!
            Sing hey,
            Lackaday!
        Let the tears fall free
For the pretty little flower
        And the great oak tree!

When she found that he was fickle,
     Was that great oak tree,
She was in a pretty pickle,
     As she well might be—
But his gallantries were mickle,
For Death followed with his sickle,
And her tears began to trickle
     For her great oak tree!

Said she, "He loved me never,
     Did that great oak tree,
But I'm neither rich nor clever,
     And so why should he?
But though fate our fortunes sever,
To be constant I'll endeavour,
Aye, for ever and for ever,
     To my great oak tree!"

THE YEOMEN OF THE GUARD

Colonel Fairfax's Ballad

Is life a boon?
     If so, it must befall,
     That Death, whene'er he call,
Must call too soon.
     Though fourscore years he give,
     Yet one would pray to live
Another moon!
     What kind of plaint have I,
     Who perish in July?
     I might have had to die,
Perchance, in June!

Is life a thorn?
     Then count it not a whit!
     Man is well done with it;
Soon as he's born
     He should all means essay
     To put the plague away;
And I, war-worn,
     Poor captured fugitive,
     My life most gladly give—
     I might have had to live
Another morn!

Jack Point and Elsie's Duet

          I have a song to sing, O!

          Sing me your song, O!

          It is sung to the moon
          By a love-lorn loon,
     Who fled from the mocking throng, O!
It's a song of merryman, moping mum,
Whose soul was sad, and whose glance was glum,
Who sipped no sup, and who craved no crumb,
     As he sighed for the love of a ladye.
          Heighdy! heighdy!
          Misery me, lackadaydee!
He sipped no sup, and he craved no crumb,
     As he sighed for the love of a ladye.

          I have a song to sing, O!

          What is your song, O?

          It is sung with the ring
          Of the songs maids sing
     Who love with a love life-long, O!
It's the song of a merrymaid, peerly proud,
Who loved a lord and who laughed aloud
At the moan of the merryman, moping mum,
Whose soul was sad, and whose glance was glum,
Who sipped no sup, and who craved no crumb,
     As he sighed for the love of a ladye.
          Heighdy! heighdy!
          Misery me, lackadaydee!

          I have a song to sing, O!

          Sing me your song, O!

          It is sung to the knell
          Of a churchyard bell,
     And a doleful dirge, ding dong, O!
It's a song of a popinjay, bravely born,
Who turned up his noble nose with scorn
At the humble merrymaid, peerly proud,
Who loved a lord, and who laughed aloud
At the moan of a merryman, moping mum,
Whose soul was sad and whose glance was glum,
Who sipped no sup, and who craved no crumb,
     As he sighed for the love of a ladye.
          Heighdy! heighdy!
          Misery me, lackadaydee!

          I have a song to sing, O!

          Sing me your song, O!

          It is sung with a sigh
          And a tear in the eye,
     For it tells of a righted wrong, O!
It's a song of the merrymaid, once so gay,
Who turned on her heel and tripped away
From the peacock popinjay, bravely born,
Who turned up his noble nose with scorn
At the humble heart that he did not prize:
So she begged on her knees, with downcast eyes,
For the love of the merryman, moping mum,
Whose soul was sad, and whose glance was glum,
Who sipped no sup, and who craved no crumb,
     As he sighed for the love of a ladye.
          Heighdy! heighdy!
          Misery me, lackadaydee!
His pains were o'er, and he sighed no more,
     For he lived in the love of a ladye.

Phoebe's Song

Were I thy bride,
Then all the world beside
  Were not too wide
    To hold my wealth of love—
Were I thy bride!

Upon thy breast
My loving head would rest,
  As on her nest
    The tender turtle dove—
Were I thy bride!

This heart of mine
Would be one heart with thine,
  And in that shrine
    Our happiness would dwell—
Were I thy bride!

And all day long
Our lives should be a song:
  No grief, no wrong
    Should make my heart rebel—
Were I thy bride!

The silvery flute,
The melancholy lute,
  Were night-owl's hoot
    To my low-whispered coo—
Were I thy bride!

The skylark's trill
Were but discordance shrill
  To the soft thrill
    Of wooing as I'd woo—
Were I thy bride!

The rose's sigh
Were as a carrion's cry
  To lullaby
    Such as I'd sing to thee,
Were I thy bride!

A feather's press
Were leaden heaviness
  To my caress.
    But then, of course, you see,
I'm not thy bride!

THE GONDOLIERS

Marco and Giuseppe's Duet

We're called *gondolieri*,
But that's a vagary,
It's quite honorary
    The trade that we ply.
For gallantry noted

Since we were short-coated,
To beauty devoted,
  Giuseppe
  Are Marco } and I;

When morning is breaking,
Our couches forsaking,
To greet their awaking
      With carols we come.
At summer day's nooning,
When weary lagooning,
Our mandolins tuning,
      We lazily thrum.

When vespers are ringing,
To hope ever clinging,
With songs of our singing
      A vigil we keep.
When daylight is fading,
Enwrapt in night's shading,
With soft serenading
      We sing them to sleep.

The Duke of Plaza-Toro's Song

In enterprise of martial kind,
    When there was any fighting,
He led his regiment from behind—
    He found it less exciting.
But when away his regiment ran,
    His place was at the fore, O—
      That celebrated,
      Cultivated,
      Underrated
        Nobleman,
    The Duke of Plaza-Toro!

When, to evade Destruction's hand,
    To hide they all proceeded,
No soldier in that gallant band
    Hid half as well as he did.
He lay concealed throughout the war,
    And so preserved his gore, O!
      That unaffected,
      Undetected,
      Well-connected
        Warrior,
    The Duke of Plaza-Toro!

When told that they would all be shot
    Unless they left the service,
That hero hesitated not,
    So marvellous his nerve is.
He sent his resignation in,
    The first of all his corps, O!
      That very knowing,
      Overflowing,
      Easy-going
        Paladin,
    The Duke of Plaza-Toro!

"Life's a Pudding Full of Plums"

Life's a pudding full of plums,
  Care's a canker that benumbs.
Wherefore waste our elocution
On impossible solution?
Life's a pleasant institution,
  Let us take it as it comes!

Set aside the dull enigma,
  We shall guess it all too soon;
Failure brings no kind of stigma—
  Dance we to another tune!
    String the lyre and fill the cup,
    Lest on sorrow we should sup.
Hop and skip to Fancy's fiddle,
Hands across and down the middle—
Life's perhaps the only riddle
    That we shrink from giving up!

The Duchess's Song

On the day when I was wedded
  To your admirable sire,
I acknowledge that I dreaded
  An explosion of his ire.
I was overcome with panic—
For his temper was volcanic,
  And I didn't dare revolt,
  For I feared a thunderbolt!
I was always very wary,
  For his fury was ecstatic—
His refined vocabulary
  Most unpleasantly emphatic.
    To the thunder
      Of this Tartar
    I knocked under
      Like a martyr;

When intently
  He was fuming,
I was gently
  Unassuming—
When reviling
  Me completely,
I was smiling
  Very sweetly:
Giving him the very best, and getting back the very worst—
That is how I tried to tame your great progenitor—at first!
  But I found that a reliance
    On my threatening appearance,
  And a resolute defiance
    Of marital interference,
  And a gentle intimation
  Of my firm determination
    To see what I could do
    To be wife and husband too
  Was the only thing required
    For to make his temper supple,
  And you couldn't have desired
    A more reciprocating couple.
    Ever willing
      To be wooing,
    We were billing,—
      We were cooing;
    When I merely
      From him parted,
    We were nearly
      Broken-hearted—
    When in sequel
      Reunited,
    We were equal-
      Ly delighted.
So with double-shotted guns and colors nailed unto the mast,
I tamed your insignificant progenitor—at last!

BOOKS ABOUT GILBERT AND SULLIVAN

THE UNDENIABLE SPARKLE AND BRILLIANCE of the Gilbert and Sullivan operas has been intensified by the sidelights cast on the subject by admiring writers. The following list of books, while by no means exhaustive, has been a source of illumination and heightened appreciation of the Savoyard world presented in this volume.

ADBURGHAM, ALISON. *Liberty's: A Biography of a Shop.* London: George Allen and Unwin Ltd., 1975.

ALLEN, REGINALD, ed. *Sir Arthur Sullivan: Composer and Personage.* New York: The Pierpont Morgan Library, 1975.

AYRE, LESLIE. *The Gilbert and Sullivan Companion.* New York: Dodd, Mead & Company, 1972.

BAILY, LESLIE. *Gilbert and Sullivan and Their World.* London: Thames and Hudson, 1973.

BINNEY, MALCOLM, PETER LAVENDER, and JAMES SPERO, eds. *The Authentic Gilbert and Sullivan Songbook: 92 Unabridged Selections from All 14 Operas Reproduced from Early Vocal Scores.* New York: Dover Publications, Inc., 1977.

BRADLEY, IAN, ed. *The Annotated Gilbert and Sullivan.* London and New York: Penguin Books, 1982.

BRAHMS, CARYL. *Gilbert and Sullivan: Lost Chords and Discords.* London: Weidenfeld and Nicolson, 1975.

BURNAND, F. C., and ARTHUR S. SULLIVAN. *Cox and Box or The Long-Lost Brothers.* Libretto and score. London: Boosey & Hawkes, n.d.

Complete Plays of Gilbert and Sullivan, The: Illustrated by W. S. Gilbert. New York and London: W. W. Norton & Co., 1976.

DARLINGTON, W. A. *The World of Gilbert and Sullivan.* New York: Thomas Y. Crowell Company, 1950.

GILBERT, W. S. *The Bab Ballads.* London: John Camden Hotten, 1869.

———. *The Bab Ballads.* Ed. by James Ellis. Cambridge: The Belknap Press of Harvard University Press, 1970.

———. *The Bab Ballads* and *Songs of a Savoyard.* London: Macmillan and Co., Limited, 1953.

GREEN, MARTYN, ed. *Martyn Green's Treasury of Gilbert and Sullivan: The Complete Librettos of Eleven Operettas / The Words and Music of One Hundred and Two Favorite Songs.* New York: Simon and Schuster, Fireside Book, 1941, 1961.

HIBBERT, CHRISTOPHER. *Gilbert and Sullivan and Their Victorian World.* New York: American Heritage Publishing Co., Inc., 1976.

WILLIAMSON, AUDREY. *Gilbert and Sullivan Opera.* London and Boston: Marion Boyars, 1953, 1982.

ACKNOWLEDGMENTS

THE POSTERS, CARDS, DRAWINGS, costume designs, record and sheet music art, documents, and other memorabilia that enliven the pages of this book come from several important collections.

We wish to thank Richard Traubner, author of numerous books and articles about the musical stage, for the use of historic Gilbert and Sullivan pictorial material from the Traubner Theatre Collection, photographed specially for this book by Steven Sloman.

Our thanks also to the Pierpont Morgan Library, whose original documents and illustrative material form one of the great Gilbert and Sullivan archives, and to Fredric Woodbridge Wilson, for his help in making the material available.

The small black-and-white drawings scattered throughout the book are from W. S. Gilbert's own *The Bab Ballads,* published in 1869. He said of them, "I have ventured to publish the illustrations . . . because, while they are certainly quite as bad as the Ballads, I suppose they are not much worse. . . . the little pictures would have a right to complain if they were omitted."